A GIRL'S GUIDE TO

KICKING
GOALS

A GIRL'S GUIDE TO
KICKING GOALS

**Steph Claire Smith
& Laura Henshaw**

murdoch books

Sydney | London

Contents

1.

Our journeys

*S*o, you bought our book! Or was it a gift? Either way, we want you to know that we've put our hearts and souls into these pages and we hope you enjoy what we have to say. We're not professional gurus (if that's even a thing), but just a couple of normal girls who grew up with normal lives and followed our dreams.

This book traces our journeys towards finding balance, happiness and acceptance of ourselves in a digital world. We wanted to share everything we've learned and everything we wish we'd known when we were growing up, to help equip you to be the most incredible young woman you can be. Please use our book as a guide to growing up in a world dominated by social media. We want you to know that being the best you can be is not about comparing yourself to anyone else: it's about embracing who you truly are inside.

STEPH

My journey

If I'm going to tell you my story, about the ups and the
downs along the path to get to where I am today, then I have
to start from the very beginning. I was born in Melbourne,
Australia, in 1994. I have an older brother, Murray, and two
loving parents, Wendy and Russell. My family has always been
incredibly supportive of me. My parents encouraged me in all
the sports and hobbies I was interested in as a little girl
and were always behind me when it came to my dream of becoming
a model. My relationship with my brother Murray has always
been strong, in fact I've never understood siblings who didn't
get along with each other. To me, Murray was superman, and
I wanted to be just like him. It's fair to say that Murray
inspired my love of team sports. He played basketball, so
I played basketball; he played netball, so I played netball.

As for my parents, my mum is quite possibly the sweetest and
most selfless person you could ever meet. We may have had
our disagreements when I was younger but now she is easily
one of my best friends and an incredible role model. My dad
is hilarious and loved by all; I give him credit for my loud
voice and confidence. He taught me to not be afraid to be
myself, and to always chase my dreams.

I attended Boroondara Park primary school, and then Balwyn
High, both public schools. When I was in primary school
I dreamed of being a model or a singer… but let's just say I
should have stuck to singing in the shower and never in front

I could eat anything I liked when I was a little girl, and so I did! I must have had a super-efficient metabolism.

of my school! Thanks to my overly supportive parents,
I thought I was an amazing singer… turns out, I wasn't.

When I was in high school I still dreamed of being a model,
but also became interested in photography and animals; I even
thought I might grow up to be a PE teacher. I was a sporty
kid: I loved netball, basketball, soccer, Little Athletics,
skipping, and the list goes on. But throughout my childhood,
even in my teens, I didn't look at playing sport as 'exercise'
or as a way of 'staying in shape' – it was just something I
did because it made me happy.

I began modelling at the age of 18 and that was when the changes started happening.

Things changed when I was around 18. I began modelling at
exactly the same time as my body was becoming curvier, and I
started working out for physical results. That was the first
time I became aware of my diet too. As a child I always had
a super-quick metabolism that meant I could eat anything and
everything and stay slim. And I can assure you, that's exactly
what I did. Funnily enough, the only insecurity I had about
my body in my teens was that my stomach was 'boyish'; I even
wished at one point that I didn't have abs! Anyway, it wasn't
until my body started to change at 18 that I began to really
look at what I was eating and focus on a 'healthier' diet. It
wasn't easy though, and the routine I'm in now didn't happen
overnight, that's for sure.

If there's one thing I would love to teach younger girls as
they grow into young women, it is that your body will change
continuously as your lifestyle changes. No one routine will
set you up for life: you need to alter it as you go. And know
that you will have ups and downs on your way.

One of my own 'down periods' was when I was 20 years old and I began modelling overseas. I had been modelling in Australia for a few years by this time and was working a lot, never having any issues with my measurements. So I was feeling confident when I moved to New York City. My confidence dropped quickly though when I discovered that the agency I had signed with a year earlier now wanted to change me. I was new to the international scene and I believed what the agency was asking of me was reasonable. I didn't fit the measurements the agency wanted, so they asked me to work on my body. I had to go into their office a couple of times a week to have my measurements checked. Being measured so often would undermine the confidence of the strongest of people, let alone an easily influenced young woman who had just moved to the Big Apple to chase her dreams.

I was already working out six days a week and eating well, so to make the changes they demanded was going to be hard...

I knew I had to take it to another level to please the agency. At this point I was already eating a healthy diet and working out almost every day, but I started working out twice a day, every day; I stopped going out with friends, I stopped eating foods that I loved. And I did lose weight, but I also lost some other things, like energy and confidence. I went back into the agency and they were happy to see that I was getting smaller, but they wanted more. I realised I couldn't keep going. I didn't feel like myself and I was unhappy. I was the thinnest I had been in years and yet I was also the most insecure I had ever been.

While I was in New York, I met a few supermodels who I had aspired to be like for years. One day at the gym I watched them pick on themselves in the mirror. I was shocked. In my eyes these girls were perfect. But then I realised I had people saying the same to me, and it dawned on me that every single person in the world has insecurities. Nobody thinks they're perfect, and nobody is perfect.

18
YEARS
OLD

24
YEARS
OLD

As a model I focused on a healthy diet and working out. But when I moved to New York, my measurements were suddenly a problem.

I left that agency and New York and returned home to Australia. I quickly got back into my usual routine of exercise, but the months of super-restrictive eating meant I struggled to work out the balance of healthy eating and exercise. So instead of just being more relaxed about what I was eating, I got into the habit of overeating or binge eating. I thought the amount I was eating was fine because it was all 'healthy' food but eating more was starting to influence my mindset. I began to feel guilty for eating so much, and then extremely disappointed in myself for doing it repeatedly. I was 'losing control'. I couldn't stop overeating; I really felt like I couldn't. I would tell myself to stop but I wouldn't listen. Sometimes I was so angry I would punish myself by restricting my eating severely, or by smashing myself at the gym or, even worse, throwing up. I was at the point where I had lost who I was as a person.

I was home, but the insecurities that I had gained living overseas had come home with me.

I had no clear direction and I wasn't working out or eating healthy for the right reasons: it was all about the physical effects. What I didn't understand at the time was that there was no weight or measurement that could make me happy while I was working out and eating for the wrong reasons.

Since this time, I have learnt that what makes me happy is focusing my mindset on healthy living. I live the way I do and make the choices I do because they make me happy; I know I'm doing right by my body. I have come a long way from that difficult period of my life but that's not to say I have it all together all the time. I still have insecurities and fall into that guilty mindset from time to time, but I've learnt to get over it and move on quicker than I used to.

When I chose to be a model I put myself in a position of being looked at and judged by others, but what took me a long time to appreciate was that models come in all shapes and sizes. Not every model can be right for a job. I started to understand that I couldn't get every job, and that being turned down from a job didn't mean I was ugly. What helped me get to this point was surrounding myself with the right people: supportive people who cared about me.

One of the special people has been my incredible friend, Laura. She always motivates me in a positive way towards healthy living. Another is my boyfriend, Josh, who is the most supportive partner I could ask for. Josh has seen me go through all my ups and downs and has been there for me when I've needed him. He keeps me grounded, that's for sure. Whenever I'm stressed he quickly reminds me how lucky I am and how silly I am for getting worked up over little things.

Now I'm confident in my own skin; I know I'm not perfect and I've come to understand that everybody has insecurities. Once you accept that, it's easier to love yourself the way you are and to see yourself as beautifully unique.

Learning to love yourself is easier said than done, which is half the reason that Keep It Cleaner (KIC) was created. Laura and I believe that looking after yourself by living a healthy lifestyle is the best way to begin to love your body for what it can do, rather than what it looks like.

These days, I still model but not full time, which has certainly helped with my mental health. My days are always different and that's something I love about what I do. If I'm not on a modelling job, I'm replying to emails, shooting for KIC, meeting with clients and business partners or travelling and just enjoying life's opportunities. I believe I have found a good balance between my work and my life. The two things are like one and I feel that I'm now fortunate enough to make decisions about my life on my own terms.

growing up was great with two sisters to hang out with! We're very different, but very close.

LAURA

My journey

Steph's journey and my journey are both special – but they're very different. Everyone's path is different, which is the way it should be. Our unique journeys, upbringings and family cultures are what make us all special.

I grew up in Melbourne. I went to a local public primary in East Ivanhoe, then Our Lady of Mercy College Catholic high school in Heidelberg. I have two amazing younger sisters, Sienna and Lucy, who I feel very lucky to have had beside me. We are all extremely different. Lucy wants to be a doctor and work in Africa, Sienna wants to be an architect, and then there's me. I'm not sure what my job title would be – part law and business student, part business owner, part model?

My parents divorced when I was 14, which is one of the most difficult things I have ever had to go through. When I look back now though, I can see that most of my pain came from worrying about what other people would think. I was worried we wouldn't be seen as a conventional and traditional family. Now I can see how much better our lives were once my parents were able to live apart. Divorce can be awful for the kids (and for the parents) and I sympathise with anyone who has been or is going through it. It's important to remember that, if your family is experiencing something like this, it doesn't mean your parents love you less: it's because they don't make each other happy. We want our parents to be happy, not least so they can be the best parents they can be. So, try to think of a difficult time as a hill on your path: it might be hard at the moment but once you get over it you'll walk down the other side and find a much happier life for your whole family.

One of the fondest memories I have from my childhood is playing sport. I was in every team. I didn't even mind being a benchwarmer – I just loved the feeling of being part of a team. I stayed active by playing sports and running with my sister Sienna up until I was 17, when I joined a gym. I was always naturally lean and athletic so joining the gym was mostly about being 'cool' and spending time there with my friends. During high school, I ate cereal every morning, fruit and yoghurt for recess, a meat and salad sandwich for lunch, cereal after school and whatever mum cooked for dinner (I would also sneak in a chocolate bar if I found a $2 coin in my dad's pants in the washing). We mostly ate home-cooked meals and I rarely took money to school for canteen lunches. I was envious of everyone's canteen lunches, but now I'm grateful that I grew up on a balanced and healthy diet.

I feel so lucky not to have had any worries or pressures about my body image while I was growing up.

I was lucky to grow up in the family I'm in, and I was lucky to go through my high school years without experiencing any pressure around body image. I never thought about diets and wasn't active on social media until I was 19, but I know this certainly isn't the case for girls today. It saddens me whenever we get emails from young girls about wanting to avoid eating home-cooked meals or to lose weight while they are still in high school. I believe that if you stay active, by playing school sport or going to the park, and if you eat well (including your mum's cooking) you will grow into your body and be fine. Dieting shouldn't be something you think about when you're still a teenager; it's more important to develop healthy habits that will carry you through to adulthood.

As a teenager I loved being in every sports team around. I went running with my sister and staying lean was easy.

I discovered Instagram when I was 19 and it opened up a whole new world to me that I had never had access to before; so much exposure to various accounts that claimed if you ate a certain way you could achieve the 'picture perfect' body. I was curious, as it was all so new to me, so I wanted to find out more. This curiosity led to an obsession with these accounts and started to also creep into my 'real life'. I began following weight-loss accounts that promoted toxic messages about body image and food. Some of the ridiculous hashtags they used were things like #eatingischeating and #nothingtastesasgoodasskinnyfeels, which I know now are wrong in so many ways, but at the time I would spend hours every day scrolling through these pages. It took over a big part of my life and I started to believe their messaging.

My unhealthy relationship with food began when I started to use social media at the age of 19.

I followed a whole mix of dieting pages – paleo, vegan, macro counting, calorie counting and raw food accounts – trying to stick to all the diets at the same time. I counted every calorie I consumed and would get mad at myself if I exceeded 1,500 calories per day. I also know now that this meant my body was always in calorie deficit and not being fuelled enough to be healthy. I remember one time when my then boyfriend made me a meal: I watched him cook using a lot of oil and, because we had only just started dating, I didn't feel comfortable sharing my food anxiety with him, so I pretended to tuck in. Really, I was just cutting the food into smaller pieces, so it would look as if I had eaten more than I did. I would cancel plans with friends because I was too worried about eating out and not being able to control what was in my food. If I did go out I would have an excuse ready as to why I wasn't eating. During this period of my life, I thought my behaviour was normal because everyone I looked up to on social media was doing the same thing. I was spending two hours a day in the gym, working out purely so I would look a certain way, rather than anything to do with how happy or healthy I was feeling.

Around the age of 21-22 I became increasingly aware that what I was doing wasn't good for my state of mind. However, it was also around then that I went overseas to model, which pushed me deeper into my unhealthy food and exercise habits. Modelling overseas was not for me. I don't have a naturally stick-thin body type and I was curvier than a lot of the girls on the international modelling scene. I was told to lose weight to reach the required 'measurements' and it wasn't long before my life was being consumed by these numbers. There was a goal weight for me to work towards: I thought if I got to this weight I would be happy with myself and my body. The funny thing was, though, when I got to this weight, it didn't make me happy at all. I just started to focus on all the other things I could still change and wondered if losing more weight would make these changes happen.

I was following a whole load of dieting pages and not going out with friends. But I thought my behaviour was normal.

Once I came back to Australia I started working to find balance in my life. My incredible friends, with Steph at the forefront, helped me reconnect with food and exercise in a healthy way. They pushed me back to the more positive relationship with my body that I'd had before I started modelling and got on social media. I cleaned out my social media accounts and deleted all the calorie-counting apps I had been using. I taught myself to look at food as fuel instead of a number. I stopped worrying about fats and carbs and instead focused on eating balanced, healthy wholefoods. I slowly came to understand that one unhealthy meal didn't mean I deserved to be punished. If I was eating healthily 80 per cent of the time, I was doing a bloody good job. If I

didn't deprive myself, and had a treat when I felt like one, I stopped binge eating and removed any guilt associated with my eating. I also changed my relationship with exercise: I began to use exercise to feel strong and empowered, and for all the energy it gave me. I don't weigh myself anymore, and I don't worry about any of my body's imperfections. I have surrounded myself with people who make me feel good about myself and don't make me feel I need to change.

What I have learnt, and what I want all girls and young women to understand, is that worrying about silly, superficial things like a thigh gap, or abs or a lifted butt won't bring you any happiness. What will make you happy is spending time with friends and family, and having a balanced and healthy relationship with food and exercise.

Steph and I started Keep It Cleaner when we got home from modelling overseas. Steph called one day to tell me she'd had a dream that we made an e-book together. It sounds funny now but that is where we got the idea to start a business! We had no idea what to do at first, so we researched everything on Google. We spent months creating and testing recipes, we styled all the photos ourselves and shot the images with a photographer friend. We look back now and giggle at how naive we were, but we're still proud of the e-book because it's a symbol of our hard work and determination. Just like everything in life, starting and believing in yourself to complete something or do something new, is the hardest part.

We had an amazing response to our e-book and it wasn't long before we launched our first Keep it Cleaner website, where we could post recipes, blogs and workouts. This was the foundation for our program. The core values behind Keep it Cleaner have always been to make healthy, easy and affordable food and exercise advice accessible to everyone. We feel very lucky that what started as a dream has become our life.

Laura xx

2.

Being social

*E*veryone's on it, every day, for hours on end. Why? Because we love learning about other people's lives: we love getting ideas for outfits, for hairstyles, for makeup, for stalking our exes, for sharing photos of our favourite breakfast, for holiday inspiration, for lifestyle inspiration, and much more. But is social media always sociable?

OUR ONLINE LIVES

Keeping it real

Social media sites like Instagram are incredible, but they're not always a positive space to spend time in. So, it's worth asking yourself why you have Instagram. Who do you follow? Why do you follow them? There are many different reasons for following different people, but what's important to recognise is if the accounts you follow end up making you feel bad about yourself. Remember that not everything you see on social media is always real; often the image you're looking at has been heavily edited. Not long ago we knew that images on billboards or in magazines had been photoshopped, but these days filters on phones and within social media sites mean that just about any image you see has probably been altered.

Here's an example, imagine you're looking at a simple photo of a woman eating her lunch at a café – it's a vibrant, colourful image, the young woman looks happy and beautiful and the food looks delicious. Is there anything wrong with this picture? Of course not. The problem is when we start comparing experiences in our own lives to the image we're looking at, without appreciating that the subject of the photo has more than likely spent hours getting the image exactly as they want it to be. Engineering the right angle, editing their hair or skin, picking a specific, flattering filter and writing a caption. What you see is not always the whole story – you're seeing the result of their hard work, rather than the spontaneous image they want you to believe you're seeing.

If you follow someone on social media who you think looks as if they have the 'perfect' life, know that that's not the case. No one is perfect, but most of us like to look as if we are! Use social media for inspiration and motivation but not as a way of comparing your life to just the parts of someone else's life that they let you see.

There is a saying that we both strongly believe in: the five people you spend the most time with will have the biggest impact on who you are as a person. This is also the case with social media. Choosing to follow certain accounts is making a choice about who you want to influence your life. Make these decisions wisely. If you are aspiring to run your own business, be a doctor, a lawyer, an artist, whatever it may be, make sure to follow people you can learn from and be proud to be influenced by.

Don't fall into the trap of comparing yourself to other people's curated online lives. They aren't always real.

STEPH I've had an Instagram account almost since the day it came out. I obviously didn't have the followers that I have now; I just used it like everyone else I saw using it. I uploaded whatever I wanted, whenever I wanted. However, I noticed quickly that I was falling into the trap of following accounts that made me feel bad about myself. I followed many popular accounts that only posted photos of 'skinny' girls or promoted weight-loss products. I started following a load of quick-fix fad diet accounts that were promoting a skinny body type, nothing to do with feeling strong or fit. I, like many others, believed everything that I saw on Instagram was real, and I became caught up in aspiring to look like the images of girls I was seeing. The truth is, I never had any way of ever looking like them, and not just because my genetic makeup is different, and I AM ME, but because they were using apps to edit their bodies or their skin, or both. I had only ever seen this happen in professional photoshoots, but now it was happening on any old photo on Instagram.

I knew that aspiring to look like an image of someone who wasn't real was an impossible task and would ultimately make me question my sense of who I was. I didn't want to feel this way, so I stopped following any accounts that fed into bad habits and I started following women who have achieved incredible things in their careers. Watching other strong and determined women doing what they love and succeeding in life is much more inspiring to me than scrolling through accounts that celebrate 'skinny' as an end goal in life.

LAURA I was a bit late to the Instagram train, being much more into Facebook. I used Instagram purely for the photo filters. I thought it was a boring app to begin with — boy, have times changed! When I started to use Instagram more regularly, I followed accounts that I thought 'inspired' me to be healthy — the same kind of fad-diet sites that Steph was looking at. It wasn't long before I was obsessing about looking like the girls on the sites, and confusing that with being inspired. I had no idea that sometimes people promoted weight-loss products they didn't actually use. And, not only that, but some images were heavily edited to make them look skinnier and 'smoother'.

Thankfully, I have grown and matured and now understand that there are no teas, lollies or tablets that lead you to your 'best body'; there is no magic pill for weight loss. The secret to a fitter, healthier body is that there is no secret. Eat well, exercise and have balance in your life. So, if you are following any accounts that are about fad diets or quick-fix weight-loss products, ask yourself: 'Is this really going to make me happier and healthier?' Most of the time you already know the answer.

THE COMPARISON TRAP

Separating online from real

Social media is an amazing space for many reasons. It's a great tool for sharing your photos; it has helped huge numbers of the younger generation start their own businesses; and it gives us access to new inspirations every day. However, we shouldn't use it without being aware that having constant exposure to enhanced and modified images can have an impact on how we see ourselves. While access to social media has opened up the world in many positive ways it has also made the world a more complicated place to grow up in. There are pressures on young women today that didn't exist 30 years ago. This can make it hard for us to accept our online presence being controlled by our parents - they didn't grow up with social media, so how could they possibly understand what it's like? This is where we come in.

Don't compare your life to others'. There's no comparison between the sun and the moon: they both shine when it's their time.

Social media has played a huge role in our lives, particularly as we transitioned from our teens to our twenties. We run our business through social media and we both have personal accounts too. Part of our business is to look good online – remember that! And if there's one thing we've learned from having to be online so much it's to always try to stay connected to the real world, and to people who care about us.

We've devised a way of telling if the time you spend online is causing an imbalance in your life. We want you to calculate for a week (or even just a day) how much time you spend online. Make a note of when and where and how often you look at social media sites. It's likely to take up a lot more time than you thought. We strongly believe that staying conscious of how much time we're spending online, stops us from getting lost in an endless loop of scrolling through images of other people's lives, subconsciously comparing ourselves to others.

It's easy to fall into the comparison trap. We look at travel images and wish we were on holiday, or we see an image of a girl in a bikini and wish we looked like that. It's easy to get caught up in this world without realising that it's taking time away from what is real in our life. If we're always online and wishing we had a life like someone else, we can forget to appreciate the life we have. This is dangerous for our mental health and overall happiness.

Be inspired, but don't be fooled into thinking that what you're seeing is the representation of true happiness. A perfect tan, a perfect bikini or a perfect setting in a beautiful location doesn't equal happiness. You won't find happiness in one place or one time in your life; happiness is something that happens as part of the journey.

We like to use an analogy for social media, one that you've probably heard before, that is 'the grass is always greener on the other side'. If you let yourself become consumed by images of other people's lives on social media and forget to draw the line in your mind to separate your own real life from curated images online, then you can start to lose touch with who you are. The grass might look greener over there; maybe you follow someone who is travelling the world with their boyfriend or girlfriend and the photos they post make their life look incredible, but remember that it's just one snapshot in time and doesn't tell the whole story. The truth is, the grass is greener where you water it. So, while you could get caught up wishing you had a life more like someone you see online, know that that person probably wishes they had a life more like someone else.

It's important to look around you every day and be grateful for what you have. Appreciate and enjoy your friends, family and experiences.

Don't be always looking at your phone. Be happy in real life, not just on the internet.

We're not the first generation to always be comparing ourselves to someone else. There is a well-established psychological theory, known as the social comparison theory, that states that personal self-worth is determined by how we compare to others. We assess our self-worth based on how we see others. The theory states that most of us can keep our jealousy in check to live our own lives but sometimes, and with the added pressure of the constant access to social media, the compulsion to compare can get the better of us.

We know what it's like when these feelings take over, so we have developed some simple steps that we use to help ground us and we want to share them with you to help you when you're feeling overwhelmed by the comparison trap.

Firstly, we focus on the fact that everyone is different, and this is what makes us special and unique. We're not just talking about what we look like - we are all obviously genetically different - but each of our journeys is unique to us. Remind yourself of this, and of how unique your body is too. Sometimes we just need to remember to celebrate our uniqueness and our own story.

Secondly, remember to appreciate that we're all at different stages in life. Imagine picking up a book and reading only the first two chapters and then trying to summarise the story. Now imagine that someone else reads 10 chapters of the same book and makes their own summary. The second person's summary would be completely different to the summary done after only two chapters. This is like life. You might find you are comparing yourself to a girl from school or university, or perhaps it's someone you follow online: it's not possible to know how far into the book of their life they have come. Have they been working for longer than you? Have they had more life experience? Are they older than you? It's most likely they will be up to a completely different chapter. So how can you compare your story to theirs?

> *Don't judge the whole of your life by the carefully chosen snippets of someone else's that they display online.*

Thirdly, use social media as a place for inspiration and motivation and empowerment, not comparison. Most accounts will only show the best five per cent of that person's life. Don't judge 100 per cent of your life against the best five per cent that they are choosing to show. Use social media as inspiration or motivation to do something healthy and invigorating - run in the bush, try an activity at the gym that you've never done before, start a hobby you've been interested in for a long time. But once you get to the gym or get started with your hobby, make sure you are doing it for you, not because you want to look like someone else.

And lastly, be aware that there may be some accounts you follow that no matter what you try telling yourself you can't stop comparing yourself to. If you notice that this is what's happening, then it's time to unfollow that account. You want your social media place to be a positive space, not one that makes you feel negatively about yourself.

We've managed to apply these rules to our lives and to Keep It Cleaner. Since launching the business and products we have been able to focus our time on creating the best program and the most delicious, healthy and easy to access products without worrying about our competitors.

We don't waste our energy on what other businesses are doing; we put all our effort into creating something awesome and setting up an amazing relationship with our customers. We keep an eye on the market to ensure we keep innovating, but our focus is on what we do best. If you don't have your own business (yet), this mindset can be applied to how you think about your school, university and/or workplace.

LAURA I used to spend so much of my time comparing myself to others. I started by judging my physical appearance against images of other girls online that I thought were more beautiful, fitter and more successful than me. Thankfully, I was able to recognise the negative influence this behaviour was having on my self-esteem and so I cleaned up my social media and stopped comparing myself to the images I was seeing online.

While I was able to moderate my desire to compare myself physically online, last year I started a new kind of comparison. This turned out to be equally damaging to my confidence. I had begun to make 'life comparisons'. I was comparing where I was in life to other people's successes. It didn't matter how much I was achieving, all I could do was focus on how much more someone else seemed to be doing. I was putting pressure on myself to achieve what women who were 10-20 years older had achieved. I loved what I was doing, but I wasn't taking time to step back and be proud of it. I was worried that if I left my office early or didn't work for a full day on the weekend I would fall behind and never reach my goals.

One morning while I was running (which is when I have most of my revelations) I had a light bulb moment and FINALLY decided that the pressure I was putting on myself and the comparisons I was making were ridiculous and that I would make a conscious effort to stop them. They weren't only stopping me from celebrating my achievements but were also taking up time I could be using to focus on my own work.

I look back now and can't believe I was comparing where I was in life to where someone much older might be, but I can also see how easy it was to fall into that trap. Now I don't worry about what others are doing, and the only comparison I make is to where I was last year. I work hard, and I push myself, but I don't measure my success by looking at somebody else.

STEPH I've always been competitive, even when I was younger I was super-competitive when it came to sports or even boyfriends! I've grown to realise that I can't do everything, and I can't win at everything. I can only strive to live my best life. In my early modelling days, I would continuously compare myself to the other girls I was shooting with. I might have been on a bikini shoot with another girl who had a completely different body type to mine, but I would still compare my body to hers. This process would leave me feeling insecure and down about myself. These feelings came through in the images – I looked uncomfortable and awkward. I knew that this behaviour had to stop if I was going to continue modelling. I now walk into shoots knowing that I work hard for the body that I have, and I'm OK with looking different to the other models in the shoot – because we're different people, after all.

Like Laura, I used to have a negative mindset when it came to my career and comparing it to what others were doing. I now tell myself to remember that I'm not going to get anywhere by having a cry about others' success. They are working hard, and they deserve whatever they are getting. And I deserve epic things too, but I must work for them in my own way.

I look at how far I've come mentally and physically, how many dream jobs I've experienced through modelling, how many beautiful countries I've visited, how many life goals I have already been able to tick off at such a young age, and how much Laura and I have done with Keep It Cleaner. And I am proud as punch.

3.
Beating the bullies

*I*t's hard to believe that social media is a relatively recent thing. It feels as if we've been using apps like Instagram forever, but the fact is that Instagram was only launched in 2010, so it's less than 10 years old. In less than a decade, Instagram and other sites and apps such as Facebook, Twitter and WhatsApp have become so popular that they have something like 2.5 billion users – close to a third of the world's population.

An unfortunate side effect of there being so many users worldwide is the number of people who use social media for the wrong reasons. We're talking specifically about bullies; those people who know that they can say any kind of nasty thing they want and remain anonymous and free of consequences. We don't know exactly why they do it, but we believe it has something to do with their own insecurities and unhappiness. The important thing to remember if you find yourself the target of online nastiness is that the bullies don't know you, so their opinions hold little weight. However, if you are being bullied by someone you know, don't ignore it. Confront them in person or speak to your parents or a teacher you trust and ask for their advice. If you see someone being bullied, or someone you know is bullying someone else, speak up. Let the bullies know that their behaviour is not acceptable and won't be tolerated.

We need to support each other online, as we would in real life, and not let the bullies win. Bullies tend to back off when they don't get the kind of reaction they are hoping for, so never sink to their level and engage in nastiness; be confident and strong and let the bullies know their opinion is not wanted or needed. And always remember you can delete online comments and block people who are trolling you; we encourage you to do this, no one needs trolls in their life.

Bullying can take many different forms and we need to be mindful of our words and actions to avoid causing someone unnecessary pain. Sometimes we can be responsible for hurting people without even realising. One of the ways we make sure that what we say and do online won't hurt someone else is to constantly remind ourselves that we don't know what anyone else is going through. We always try to be kind, empathetic and sensitive. Even a small comment that seems insignificant can be hurtful if it plays on someone's insecurities. We never want to make someone upset so we try to always be aware of our actions. We want the people around us to feel good. And we promise you that making someone happy will make you feel happy too. So much happier than if you cause them pain.

STEPH Having over a million followers on social media really opened the gates for the keyboard warriors to comment on my life. This bothered me when my followers first started growing; I didn't expect it and wasn't prepared for all the attention. Now when I get negative comments I remind myself that the online bullies don't know me. And I know that they would never say what they say to me online if they saw me in person. People tend to put someone else down because they're jealous, or because they have their own insecurities. It's very common for people to pick on others because they think it will make them feel better about their own problems, when really it doesn't: it's just a horrible thing to do.

> *Be kind to those close to you. Even a throwaway remark can be harmful if it plays on someone's insecurities.*

LAURA Social media makes bullying easy, because the bullies can hide behind a keyboard and a fake name. They write things that they would never say in person. I found that once I had a significant number of followers, people forgot I was a real person with actual feelings and they would write nasty things thinking I wouldn't read what they wrote. But of course, I did! I would get upset and feel hurt until I realised that the people who were writing mean things didn't know me. The more I reminded myself of this, the quicker I could brush off their negativity. If I happen to know the person who is saying awful things about me then I tend to just feel sad for them. The fact they take time to comment or post something negative is on them! I don't waste my time with it. I brush it off and call someone who makes me feel good about myself (usually Steph or my boyfriend, Dalton).

I'm not saying this process is always easy. It can be difficult to get the balance right between valuing the opinions of others and knowing which opinions don't carry any weight. It is important to value the opinions of the people you love, respect and care about. However, people who don't know or care about you are less likely to have your best interests at heart. A hurtful comment might take the form of a subtle dig or a discouraging message; it might be condescending in nature or a criticism of something you've done. The trick to not letting the negativity get to you is to examine the comment for its motives. If it's a negative message, then it's more than likely coming from a selfish place and is not worthy of your time or feelings. We can't please everyone, and we shouldn't exhaust ourselves trying. The most important thing is to live our lives in a way that makes us happy and fulfilled.

When I receive 'advice' from strangers online I listen, thank them and then I do what I think is best for me. Listening to my gut feeling about what to do, instead of what others wanted me to do, was how I was able to start my first health blog, Food Fit and Repeat. I used to get a lot of negative messages and comments that made me doubt myself. Some of these messages were from people who I thought were my friends. They tried to brush off their comments by saying they were joking, but I let it get to me. I would tell myself that no-one would want to read it, or no-one would care. I had to work hard to overcome the negativity and believe in myself. I had to keep reminding myself that I was doing this for me, not for anyone else.

There will ALWAYS be people who will try to hold you back, so establish a balance within yourself about how much value you're placing on other people's opinions and how much you're listening to your own gut feeling. Starting my blog was the best thing I ever did and has led me to where I am today. I'm proud that I followed my instincts instead of always believing what others thought of me. You are the only one who really knows what you want to do with your life. Only you know what you are truly capable of and what you can achieve - don't let anyone tell you otherwise.

BELIEVE IN YOURSELF

Get confident!

Have you ever noticed a person stride into a crowded room with their shoulders back and their eyes looking proudly straight ahead? Everyone stops and stares because this is what confidence looks like. This person may not be the most classically beautiful person in the room but that doesn't matter, they look engaging and intriguing. They command attention with their confidence.

Confidence is a beautiful and empowering trait and we believe that everyone deserves to feel confident in themselves; but we know that this isn't always an easy thing to achieve. Feeling self-assured doesn't come naturally to everyone, but it's something that can be practised and improved upon. We'll talk later about being confident in your body when you exercise and being confident with your food choices but here we wanted to talk in general terms about trusting in yourself and building your confidence. Believing in yourself can be one of the hardest things in the world to do, especially if you have ever had issues with your body or you have been bullied, or if you've suffered some other trauma that has dented your self-esteem. It can be tough; but trust us when we say, it is so extremely important to do the work.

If you want others to believe in you and what you do, you need to believe in it first. You need to trust that you are capable. For example, when you go for a job interview, the person interviewing you needs to know that you can do the job

Our top tips for boosting your confidence:

◊   Acknowledge your victories, big or small. All your wins should be recognised.

◊   Switch off from social media for 48 hours.

◊   Book in time with your favourite people: watch a movie, go for a walk together, share a meal. Positive and supportive influences in your life make you feel good about yourself.

◊   Practise looking in the mirror and telling yourself 'I am enough and I am worthy'.

◊   Put your shoulders back and hold your head high. Even if you're not feeling confident, when you stand tall and project confidence you will start to believe it.

◊   Put on your favourite song, turn it up loud and dance.

◊   Remind yourself that you are unique. There is no one quite like you, so be proud.

you applied for – so you need to confidently assure them that you can. If you don't believe in yourself, then your nerves will take over and your doubts and insecurities will be obvious to the interviewer. You can't ask someone to believe in you if you doubt yourself. So trust yourself and let it shine through.

Confidence doesn't come easy. For many of us it's about hard work and commitment. Sometimes we need to build a sense of worthiness – we're not always born with it. Confidence is not about being beautiful or successful or popular. None of these things are the answer to confidence, because confidence comes from within. Building confidence means looking at what's real in life. Your family, your true friends, your pets, your passions, your experiences – these are the things that keep you from being distracted by what's not real. Take time away from the online world to work out what is real to you and always remember to tell yourself that you are enough. You are worthwhile.

LAURA My own path to confidence has been quite a journey, but thanks to the support of the incredible people around me, Steph especially, I have grown to believe in myself and now I'm a lot more confident in everything I do. Don't get me wrong – I'm not always on top of the world; I don't think anyone is. One of the things that always tests my confidence is public speaking. To help calm my nerves there are a few things I do before I get up and speak. Firstly, I always make sure I'm prepared. If I have done everything in my power to do the best job I can, then I remind myself of this. It's the same process I go through for an exam. I could stress out and lose focus, or I can focus on knowing that I have prepared as best as I can. Secondly, I repeat a few lines in my head. I tell myself 'I can', 'I am capable' and 'I am enough'. Thinking confident thoughts will translate to confident feelings. Thirdly, I remind myself that no one is ever 100 per cent ready for anything and the only way to test if I can do something is to push myself out of my comfort zone. I'm where I am in my career because I challenge myself to say 'yes', and then I learn from the experience. It's like starting a new job; you can feel overwhelmed and intimidated but it's not long until it becomes second nature.

STEPH I take after my loud and confident dad, so I've always had a certain level of confidence; but that's not to say that I haven't had my self-esteem knocked over the years. I've had times when I've felt I wasn't good enough. One thing I learnt through modelling though was that confidence shines through. If there are two equally beautiful models vying for the same job and one model is feeling strong and self-assured and the other one is feeling awkward and full of self-doubt, then the model with the confidence will more than likely get

the job. I understand that it can be difficult to jump into a situation that requires confidence when you're feeling nervous or unsure of yourself. But I've learnt to trust myself and be comfortable in my own skin. I live a healthy lifestyle and I know that I look after myself. Feeling this way, I can walk into a casting or onto set with confidence, and it always turns out better than when I'm feeling unsure of myself. My advice is to find the things about yourself that you're proud of and concentrate on them. Tell yourself you're amazing, you have unique skills and you CAN do what you put your mind to. Believe in yourself. Stand up for what you believe in. Put your shoulders back and walk into that next meeting, exam, interview or party with your head held high.

4.
Your body
changes

*I*t's a crazy time when puberty hits and suddenly your body changes. We like to think of puberty as a rollercoaster, because it's certainly a wild ride. Due to our unique genetic makeup we all go through puberty at different stages and we all have our own unique experiences. For some of us it's the physical changes that we notice first: we grow taller or curvier, or more muscular. For some, it's the pimples. For others, it's all about navigating the heightened emotions that seem to take over when hormones hit. It might feel weird, but these are all normal changes that can occur repeatedly. Puberty isn't over in the space of a month or two; it's a process that can take years. The best thing you can do is relax and enjoy the ride.

STEPH I didn't get my period until I was 15. Lucky for me, I got my period on the same day as one of my best friends, so we were able to share the experience and support each other through the first time. Getting my period was about the only time anything related to puberty was in sync with my friends. I had another best mate who developed breasts at 12 years old, while I didn't start developing breasts or hips until I was 18. Always remember that these changes happen to everyone at different ages and at different rates.

Going from being a lanky teenager to a curvy woman was scary for me at first. I couldn't understand why I was gaining weight in places I never had before; and I was getting cellulite where I never had it before. I was eating a lot healthier than I had as a teenager, so it was a difficult transition. It didn't help that a lot of these changes started occurring just after my first year of modelling when my body was under so much scrutiny. I had been so confident in my body up until this point, so I had to work hard to accept all the changes. Cellulite became my biggest, and still is my biggest, insecurity. I've learnt to worry about it less and less though, because there's not much you can do about it and some people just have it more than others! Instead I concentrate on what my body is good at. I know that I'm strong and healthy and I have nothing to be embarrassed or ashamed about. I've just learned to live with it.

LAURA I was always a lanky kid and, like Steph, went through puberty late in high school. I hated it at first because I was envious of my friends' beautiful curves. I wanted to be curvy, with hips and boobs, but my friends wanted to be thin and lanky like me. It's funny how we always seem to want what we don't have!

I eventually went through puberty and experienced the kinds of changes my friends had been through. Like Steph, I also put on weight, which felt strange at first, but I just kept reminding myself that my body was going through a natural process and that's a beautiful thing.

Our bodies are getting ready to be able to have a baby, which is bloody amazing and should be celebrated. Puberty happens to everyone, it's a part of life, and a beautiful one at that.

Changes in our bodies during puberty can be upsetting if we're not ready to look different. It can be confusing when our lifestyle stays the same but our body starts behaving as if we've changed. It's important to remember that your body will change throughout much of your life, particularly, for most, between the ages of 15 and 25. Do you feel as if your head is too big for your body? Are you towering over your school mates? Or are you constantly wondering when it's going to be your turn for a growth spurt? There are millions of young women in the world who can relate to you, so know that you are not alone.

To avoid being overwhelmed, we think it helps to write down some of the physical changes you've noticed in your body. Make a list. Do these things bother you? Think about why they bother you, if they do. Now think about why these changes have occurred. Understanding the reason for the physical changes is a good way of appreciating how amazing your body really is. It might feel weird to begin with but try telling yourself every day that you love the things you've put down on your list. Channel your mind into thinking positive thoughts about your body. Before long you'll notice that you're more accepting of the things that once made you uncomfortable.

Changes in my body:

1. _____

2. _____

3. _____

4. _____

5. _____

PERIODS:
Our bodies at work

One of the most significant changes to a girl's body during puberty is starting periods. This can happen as early as nine years of age, or as late as 16; but for most girls it happens between 11 and 13. No doubt you remember the first time you got your period. You probably had many mixed emotions about the changes to your body; it may have felt exciting, or scary, or confusing; but the most important thing to tell yourself, through the emotional ups and downs, is that your period is your body doing exactly what it was designed to do. This may seem like cold comfort when our emotions make us angry, frustrated, or irrationally sad. Or when period pain leaves us curled up in a ball on the floor. That's when we need our supportive family, great friends, and understanding partners to step in and give us a hand (or a shoulder to cry on).

For some women their periods are light and short and cause little discomfort. For others it's a totally different story and they suffer through heavy bleeding and intense cramping. Unfortunately, it's the luck of the draw. One thing we all have in common when we get our periods is the general feeling of 'bleurgh'. We're tired and irritable and less motivated than usual. This is completely natural and normal. And while it's easier said than done, it's important to go easy on yourself when it's that time of the month.

The following is a list of our favourite things to do when we're having an 'off day':

◊ Invite your best friends over for homemade popcorn and movies. Surround yourself with the people who make you smile. (Don't give in to lots of junk food, instead stack up on healthy treats – you'll feel so much better afterwards.)

◊ Cook your favourite healthy recipe to share with your family or friends.

◊ Go for a walk in the sunshine (vitamin D and fresh air can make us feel a million times better). If you have a dog, take them along too.

◊ Go for a swim in the ocean (this is Laura's favourite).

◊ Read a fabulous book. Ask a friend for a recommendation or re-read one of your favourites.

◊ Run a bath and spoil yourself with some mineral salts and scented candles.

STEPH Shortly after I got my first period, around the age of 15, I started taking the contraceptive pill. I was on the same pill for six years before I decided I wanted a break to see if it would help reduce my moodiness. For a year after coming off the pill I didn't get my period. During this time, I started to get hormonal acne around my jawline; I'd never had acne like that before, so I went to my GP. My doctor suspected I had Polycystic Ovary Syndrome (PCOS) and recommended an ultrasound. Without going into too much confusing detail, it's a condition caused by elevated male hormone levels. There's no cure but there are ways to manage the symptoms. My GP recommended going back on the pill to help my skin and to regulate my periods. I did that, but I still suffered wild hormonal swings. I wanted to try something different to see if it could help my moods. I started seeing a Chinese doctor for acupuncture and I'm amazed at the improvement. He recommended I stop the pill and begin taking specially-formulated herbs. Two months after starting acupuncture and herbs and coming off the pill I got my period. I cried, I was so happy! Having my period is important because it means my body's working! I can't say I'm back to being regular but I'm getting my period and feeling better, so I'm appreciating each month as it comes. Note: I'm not saying that everyone who has PCOS should get acupuncture - everyone is different. Personally, I found it helpful to research as much as possible online and talk to various professionals. It's important to learn as much as you can about what's going on with your body.

LAURA I'm one of the unlucky ones who has long, heavy and painful periods. I get extremely grumpy and very hungry for a few days before my period starts and then feel tired and rundown for the first few days of my period. I used to push myself with my usual routines on the first two days of my cycle, but I would always feel sick. These days I LISTEN TO MY BODY. I now take a few days off exercise when my period starts. If I'm feeling OK, I might go for a walk or a gentle jog but often I do nothing. A few days' break from working out won't undo any of your progress. If your body is asking you to rest, let it. Everyone has 'off days' and that is completely fine. You're not alone. On these days do something that lets your body rest and makes you feel good.

BE YOUR BEST SELF

Love the skin you are in

The insecurities we have about our bodies don't just hit when we go through puberty. People of all ages, both men and women, can develop insecurities about the way they look at any point in their lives. No two people have the same reasons for feeling the way they do about their bodies. Coming to a place of acceptance about who you are is a complex process, and one that has many influencing factors. But one of the things we've found most shocking lately is the age at which young girls are starting to criticise their appearance. Children as young as five are becoming concerned about the way they look and what they're eating. Little children, whose bodies are growing and changing every day, should only be concerned about what game they're going to play next. Not what they look like doing it. We feel like this kind of thing is a sign that we need to concentrate on what really matters. We need to stop being so critical of ourselves and celebrate what's great about us. If we're healthy and our bodies are letting us do the stuff we love doing, then we're lucky! The 'perfect' appearance does not exist. Nobody is perfect.

If you're exercising regularly and eating a balanced and nutritious diet, then you're doing the best you can for your body and mind. Channel your mind into thinking positively and it won't be long before you will find more and more that you love about yourself. Remind yourself of the things your friends and family compliment you on, and the next

time somebody says something nice to you, say thank you and believe it. Be proud of the effort you're putting into being your best self, accept that everyone is different and love the skin you're in.

STEPH I was insecure about my stomach when I was younger because I was so sporty and had abs. I thought it made me look like a boy. Goes to show that people can be insecure about anything, right? I've grown to realise that I am fortunate to have the stomach that I do, and I don't mind looking muscly anymore because it makes me feel strong and powerful. Yes, there are things that I am still insecure about, but I try to ignore them by focusing on the things I love about myself. We both like actress Emma Stone's note to herself: to be kind and treat herself in the same gentle way she'd treat a daughter.

Next time you look in the mirror and are tempted to put yourself down, look again and tell yourself what you love about your body instead.

LAURA My body shaming started around the time I started looking at social media. I would look at girls online who I thought had great bodies, and mine looked nothing like theirs. I used to hate my dimples because I thought they meant I was 'too big', and I hated the bum I grew because it meant my modelling measurements were way too big. I spent a few years continuing to hate these changes, and then slowly and gradually learnt to love my own body and celebrate my dimples and bum. Something that helped me finally embrace the bodily changes of puberty is how unique we all are. We all have different genes, so there is no way your body can ever look like or go through the same changes as someone else's. So instead of letting it get to you, and not seeing your body for the beautiful thing that it is, change your mindset! Celebrate your unique body and focus on loving parts of it, instead of focusing on the bits you don't like so much.

As an exercise in self-confidence, we want you to write down the things you love about yourself. Make it a mixture of things. Think about your skills and abilities, your personal traits, your interests, as well as your physical appearance and capabilities. You might start with only a few, and that's OK, because we want you to keep coming back to it when you think of more. Enjoy the feeling as you watch the list grow.

5.
Relationships
& role models

W e're more and more aware of how the people we follow and admire online have an influence on us; however, even more powerful and influential are the people we choose to surround ourselves with. It's important to take time to look around and ensure that the people in your life are positive influences. Surrounding yourself with great friends, honest lovers and impressive role models is a sure-fire way to feel confident, stay focused and be the best you can be.

CHOOSING THE
RIGHT RELATIONSHIPS

Say goodbye to toxic people

Identifying toxic people in our lives isn't always easy. In some cases, it can take years to appreciate that someone doesn't have our best interests at heart. Toxic relationships can be based on control or jealousy or just an undermining lack of support and understanding. The key to surviving this sort of toxic relationship and coming out stronger and more self-assured, is to make the decision to end the relationship as soon as you can see it's having a negative influence on your life. Don't sustain a relationship thinking you can change the person, and don't feel guilty about cutting people out of your life if they are making you unhappy. It's an unfortunate fact that you will come across people who aren't truly happy for your successes; remember, this is less about you than it is about them. On the flipside, when you find friends who have your back 100 per cent, then hold on to these precious jewels with all your might.

There are different ways to end a relationship that is based on negativity. You can confront the person directly and tell them how you feel, letting them know that you won't be in contact anymore. Or, if you think it's not feasible that this person can be completely cut out of your life, or you find the thought of confrontation too stressful, then gradually reduce the amount of time and energy you spend on this person until it's at a point that you feel comfortable.

If you're struggling with a relationship you think might be toxic, ask yourself these questions:

◊ Do they truly want you to be happy? Do they seem genuinely excited and pleased when you are happy, or is their excitement lessened when you're in a happy state?

◊ Are they happy and supportive when it comes to your successes? Are they quick to congratulate you or do they hold back on their praise?

◊ Do they make efforts to control you?

◊ Do you feel good about yourself when you are around them?

◊ Does the relationship feel equal? That is, is there an equal amount of time spent on each person?

◊ Do you trust them?

Genuine friends should make you feel good about yourself. They are happy for you when you're doing well and there with honest advice and support when things aren't going so well. They don't try to have any control over your life and are happy just to let you be yourself.

DON'T GO CHANGING

Staying true to yourself

A great relationship is built on acceptance and understanding. Nobody is perfect, which is why the best relationships are the ones where each person is aware of the other's flaws but accepts and admires them anyway. A relationship that allows you to be vulnerable with the other person, but still feel loved and supported, is a truly strong bond.

Be yourself. Everyone else is already taken.

This leads us to one of the biggest (and very common) mistakes we can make in our relationships: when we try to change who we are to please someone. If we measure our own self-worth by what someone else wants us to be, then our self-esteem plummets. If you're not able to be yourself around someone then you live in a constant state of uncertainty about how to behave. If someone doesn't want you to be who you really are then this isn't someone you need in your life.

There are incredible relationships out there waiting just for you. Remind yourself that if we were all the same then the world would be a very boring place.

MORE THAN FRIENDS

Falling in love

If there's one relationship above all that requires trust, honesty and vulnerability to succeed, it's your intimate, romantic relationship. Here is where we all deserve to feel safe and loved for who we truly are. Nothing compares to the feeling you get when you're with someone who loves you for you, flaws and all. Every romantic relationship you have will be different. Each partner will treat you differently: they might like different things about you, or want to do different things with you. The more relationships you have, or the longer you are in a committed relationship, the more you will start to learn about what you like and what you don't. Some relationships grow and evolve, and some don't. If you notice you're unhappy in a relationship don't stay because you're scared of being lonely. There's nothing wrong with being single and focusing solely on your own happiness.

STEPH I've always been a relationship person; I like having a boyfriend. I had a few relationships before Josh. And, even though he was there all along, we both look back and agree that we got together at the right time and needed to experience our other relationships first. I have known Josh for half my life and one of the best things about our relationship is that we know each other so well. I have been myself from the beginning, so I know he loves me for me. It wasn't always this way with ex-boyfriends. In the past I let myself be treated in a way I would never accept today.

I was young when I lost my virginity to an older boy; and, while I don't regret my first time, I look back now and realise that I was going along with everything my boyfriend wanted without asking myself if it was what I wanted. In my opinion your first time should be with someone that you love, and you should never feel pressured in any way to do anything you don't want to.

My next partner and I were together for two and a half years, during which time I learnt a lot about myself. It wasn't a healthy relationship and we had serious issues with trust. Our lack of trust in each other created conflict and it felt like we were constantly fighting. As it turns out he was cheating on me for a good deal of our relationship. At the time this was horribly painful, but now when I look back I think it taught me to not be afraid of being alone. If I hadn't found out about his cheating, we might have tried to stick it out when we were clearly not right for each other.

And now there's Josh. In a way he has been there all along, it just took some living to realise that he is the one for me. I get a lot of girls asking me how I can trust Josh. The answer probably isn't very satisfying: because I just do. I trust him with all my heart because he has never done anything to make me feel otherwise. I trust that he is a good person. I believe he would never hurt me and we always try to be as honest with each other as possible. It's true that he follows gorgeous girls online, and he 'likes' their photos; but he also tells me multiple times a day how beautiful he thinks I am and how lucky he thinks he is. When we first started dating Josh was working at a nightclub every Saturday. His job had him working with lots of beautiful women. At first, I was jealous, but I kept telling myself that the reason I fell in love with Josh was because he is confident, charming and loves being social. I couldn't let my jealousy get in the way of Josh being himself. He was also being equally reasonable with me in my work. He trusts me to be professional and doesn't let any jealous feelings get in the way of my work. Our relationship is based on trust and mutual respect, which frees us both to love unconditionally. Josh and I have been through a lot together, and it's not always easy. But the truth is I feel happy, beautiful and loved when I'm with him.

LAURA I am also lucky to be in a loving relationship with a beautiful partner who cares about me and supports me. However, this hasn't always been the case. In high school I seemed to like the cool guys, who were usually a bit on the jerk side. I had a lovely boyfriend when I was 15/16 but when that relationship ended I found myself trying to fit into a 'cool' scene. I would dress and act in a way that I thought would impress the boys and I was terrified of being alone. I was obsessed with having a full face of makeup and I would never let any of these 'cool guys' see me without it. I would even sleep in my makeup, which was so silly looking back on it now. In hindsight I can see how damaging this was for my confidence and my sense of self, constantly trying to be something or someone that I wasn't. It's a huge relief to have let all that go.

One of the few things I am proud of from that time is that I never gave in to the pressures of doing something sexual just so a guy would like me. I have my Catholic school to thank for that. If you're feeling pressure from a boyfriend to have sex and he isn't respecting your decision to wait, then he's not the right guy. Having sex for the first time should be on your terms. It's a special thing and you get to choose when this happens. There are lots of beautiful boys out there who will respect this; one of these is the guy for you. And when you do start having sex remember that your sex life is exactly that – yours! It doesn't define who you are and shouldn't come with any labels. If I had any advice to give from this point in my life, it would be: don't be in a relationship with anyone who you can't be yourself with; and remember there is more to life than boys.

I started dating a great, kind boy after Year 12. We were together for five years and, even though the relationship didn't work out, he helped me step away from my wild partying ways and refocus on my studies and career. I will always be grateful to him – he made me feel comfortable about who I was and confident to trust that I was enough.

My partner, Dalton, and I had known each other as acquaintances for a little while before we became good friends. From this point our relationship grew into what it is today. I am endlessly grateful to be in a relationship now where I feel valued, loved and supported, as well as being crazy in love. I still get butterflies when we kiss! Dalton fully supports my career and is my absolute rock. He has a special mantra he repeats to me whenever I'm suffering from self-doubt: 'You are kind, you are beautiful, you are powerful, you are Laura.' It's simple and perfect and makes me feel better every time.

I know there is no 'perfect' relationship, and Dalton and I will fight every now and then because we are both passionate people, but at the end of the day we always know we still love each other.

The following is a list of traits that we believe should be part of everyone's relationship:

◊ Trust

◊ Honesty

◊ Equality

◊ Being able to be yourself

◊ Feeling safe and supported in what you do

◊ Feeling unconditionally loved

LEARNING FROM THE BEST

Role models

R ole models are the people in your life who set a great example for you to learn from and gain inspiration. A role model can be anyone and any age; it might be your mum or dad, a business person, a close friend, or just someone you know who makes inspiring choices. We've found role models to be invaluable contributors to who we are today, and we want you to think about who your role models are or could be. You can take different inspiration from different people: your mum might be a role model when it comes to how you treat people, but a famous athlete might be someone you admire when it comes to fitness. You can have as many or as few role models as you like. It's about what inspires you to be the best version of yourself.

STEPH If you had asked me who my role models were when I was a teenager, my answer would have been very different to today. In high school I was incredibly influenced by the older 'cool' girls. If they used a Country Road bag instead of a backpack, so did I; if they wore a faded, old PE uniform that was two sizes too small, I would use my pocket money at the school uniform shop to look the same. I feel grateful that I didn't have Instagram back then – I'm sure I would have been influenced by the wrong people, or at least focused on superficial things. I also used to look up to many successful and beautiful models and, while I still respect these women for their hard work in the modelling industry,

I have certainly started to move more towards women outside the modelling industry who are doing amazing things. One role model who deserves a mention above all others is my mum. I've always had a good relationship with her, but when I was younger I didn't appreciate all she was doing to shape who I've become. I assumed a role model was someone who had the career that I wanted; I didn't realise that my mum was the one who was teaching me about important core values. Mum is selfless, loving, supportive and proactive. I admire her strength and I hope I can be like her when I'm a mum.

I aspire to be happy, healthy and good at what I do; so, I take inspiration from people I see trying to achieve these goals. I'm always reminding myself that having a role model is not about wanting to be that person; it's about respecting them for their achievements or who they are as a person and wanting to better yourself in your own way.

LAURA   Just like Steph, my role models have changed as I've grown up, with the exception of my mum, who has always been someone I've looked up to, and even more so as I've grown. Mum taught me about hard work and sacrifice, and to put the people you love first. She instilled in me the importance of education and to be learning and challenging myself always.

I have many role models in my life now, for many different reasons. I look up to some for their optimism and capacity to make others happy; others I admire for their business success; and others for their cool head under pressure and their ability to deal with stress. I draw inspiration from each person depending on what I need. One thing they all have in common though, is that they are strong, independent and empowering people. They make me want to be the strongest woman I can be. If I ever start to doubt myself, I think of Steph: she is incredibly good at focusing on her own goals and not worrying about what anyone else is doing. In business, I look to Boost Juice founder and franchiser, Janine Allis, for inspiration. Janine is one of the strongest women I have ever met; so, whenever we hit a hurdle with KIC I ask myself what Janine would do.

6.

Manage time:

manage stress

The busier you get, the more organised you need to be. Being organised doesn't come naturally to everyone but it's something that everyone should strive for. On the days when it seems you have a million things to do, it can quickly feel so overwhelming that you want to give up and do nothing. No matter who we are, we all have those days. Take a deep breath; getting through a packed working day is achievable, you just need to plan your time. There's nothing more satisfying than getting to the end of a busy day and looking back at all the things you have achieved. The feeling of accomplishment motivates you for tomorrow and you find you can get through more than you thought possible.

WHEN LIFE GETS BUSY

Manage your time

Everybody is busy these days. We squeeze in work, study, socialising, exercise, travel; plus, we all need some time to ourselves. We've put together some of our favourite time management tips to help you get through whatever you've got going on.

GET A DIARY

LAURA This might seem obvious, but I went without one for a few years. When I finally bought a diary again, I couldn't imagine how I had survived without it. I used to put myself under such unnecessary pressure to remember everything in my head, then I'd be angry at myself when I forgot things. Writing things in a diary takes the pressure off. As soon as something comes up I note it down in my diary.

STEPH I was so used to having a diary at school that I just continued using one when I finished. I would be completely lost without my diary. I still use a hard copy book, which is just personal preference over an online diary. I write EVERYTHING in my diary: meetings, coffee dates, workouts, appointments, reminders, to-do lists and more.

MAKE A TO-DO LIST

LAURA I was never much of a list person until I started trying to manage our Keep it Cleaner (KIC) workload, university studies and my personal training course all at once. Now, I can't live without my lists. Every morning I get up and write down my list for the day and tick it off as I get through it. If anything unexpected comes up, I simply add it to the end of the list and stay focused on my task at hand. If I don't get through it all, I just add any points I didn't get through to my list for the next day. This helps me sleep too - I know I haven't forgotten anything.

STEPH I have always been a 'to-do' list person. I find them incredibly helpful when I've got a lot on. Lists make sure I don't miss anything. I also find it satisfying to go back and check my lists to make sure that it's all done and ticked off.

GET UP EARLY

LAURA It's amazing how much time you have in the day if you get up early. I find if I oversleep I feel lethargic and unable to catch up all day. I try to get up at 6.30-7am every day and get my workout done early, so I can start my work day by 9.30am. Just remember to go to bed early enough to ensure you get 7-8 hours' sleep each night.

STEPH I used to love sleeping in. Now I feel upside down if I sleep in (not on weekends or holidays, of course). Sometimes it feels as if there aren't enough hours in the day, so I like to get up early and make the most of my time. I like to start my day with a workout and a good breakfast. Usually my working day starts between 8-10am which means I need to be up and about before that; but, as Laura said, getting enough sleep is important. So I always make sure I get to bed at a reasonable time at night.

FIND BALANCE

Balance is paramount in all areas of our lives. You need balance in your diet and exercise, you need balance in your relationships, and you need balance in your life to avoid burnout. We found that balance was essential for us during our end of school exams and at university, and even more so now that we're running our own business and managing our careers.

LAURA Something that has always worked for me during any busy period is making sure that, no matter what, I have time off to enjoy myself once a week. In Year 12 this was a Friday or Saturday night. I just made sure I was at home in bed by about midnight, so I could still get up and study the next day. These days I make sure I have one full day off (usually Sunday) to help me recharge for the week ahead. I find getting away from work can be a great way to re-motivate myself to give 100 per cent again the next day.

STEPH Life is super-busy. I can get very stressed when I'm behind on emails, or I've missed a workout, or cancelled on a friend, or even just been behind on house chores! But I find this stress usually pops up when I'm off balance; when I've been focusing too much on one part of my life and not enough on the rest. For me, staying on top of my workload is just as important as looking after my health and spending time with those I love. I used to struggle to fit everything in and found it especially hard to get all my workouts done. But then Laura taught me to schedule. She encouraged me to treat my workouts like an appointment and put them in my diary. Now I schedule everything, from coffees with friends, to business meetings, to taking Ari (my dog) for a walk. It's all important, and it's all got to be done to keep me balanced and happy.

Everyone's balance will be different and it can take some time to work out what is right for you, but there's one thing we know everyone needs and that's 'me time' every single week. Think of it as like sleep. Without a good night's sleep, you're tired all day and not able to perform at your best.

Our minds need downtime too. Take the time to find a quiet place and clear your mind. We guarantee you'll come back with a renewed focus and more energy.

PRIORITISE

The reality is that no matter how hard we try, we can't do it all. You only have so many hours in a day and only so much energy you can give. This is why you need to spend time working out your priorities. It will make saying 'no' a little easier and it lessens the guilt you feel if you know something isn't on top of your priority list. Write your priorities down. We've found that if you have a clear list written out, it's easier to organise your time and spend your energy on the parts of your life that are most important. Once you write the list, go over your diary for the week and make sure you are using your time wisely.

We love this idea from model and actor Cara Delevingne: When you have balance in your life, work becomes an entirely different experience. There is a passion that moves you to a whole new level of fulfilment and gratitude.

SET BOUNDARIES

It took us both a long time to learn to set boundaries for ourselves. The sort of boundaries we're talking about here help us achieve balance in our lives. We like to refer to them as 'life boundaries'. They might be different for everyone, but they are a vital part of looking after yourself and making the most of your time. Look at your boundaries as a set of 'life rules' or guidelines for happiness.

Laura's life boundaries:

◊ Stop working by 8pm every night (at the latest). This helps me fully wind down before bed, so my mind isn't running overtime when I lie down to sleep.

◊ Have one full day off work each week. This lets me reset for the week ahead and gives me something to look forward to during the week. It also means I get to spend time with my family and friends.

◊ Get active five or six days a week. My 30-45 minutes of exercise every day is my 'me time'; it energises me and clears my mind. I think of my exercise as a form of meditation so it's about my body and mind.

◊ Switch off from social media at night.

Steph's life boundaries:

◊ No phones during dinner, a movie or in bed. A huge part of my day is spent on my phone for work, so it's important for me to switch off and have real conversations.

◊ No more than one cancellation on a friend per week. I would love this to be zero, but my job is unpredictable and I need to be able to adapt. Keeping this rule in place reminds me how important it is to make time for my friends and family.

◊ Work out at least five times a week. My workouts keep me feeling fab and fit, but they also keep me in a healthy headspace. I start to feel lethargic later in the week if I haven't stayed active.

MANAGING YOUR STUDY

How to plan your time

I f you're still at school or in further education, then you need a study plan. There's no one-size-fits-all solution and different techniques work for different people. The only guaranteed 'technique' for success is hard work. Put simply, if you find a way of studying that suits you and you work hard, you will succeed!

STEPH   Studying doesn't come easily to me! I have a bad habit of putting it off until the last minute. After using my 'last minute' revision technique to get through my exams in Year 11, I realised I needed to be more organised for my end of school exams. I'm a visual learner, so I used diagrams to help me remember. I would draw them out onto big sheets of paper or bright sticky notes and pin them up all over the house. I also did mini tests with my friends and family and printed out old exams for practice. When it comes down to it, there's no avoiding the fact that study is hard work!

LAURA   I was lucky to be able to do a Year 12 subject in Year 11; which meant I could practise different study techniques and test what did and didn't work for my final year subjects. For my end of school exams I took English, Maths Methods, Biology, French, Human Health and Development, and PE. Most of my subjects were rote learning subjects, which meant my study technique involved a lot of memorising.

The following methods worked for me:

◊ Typing out my handwritten notes from each topic and printing them out.

◊ Going through my notes with a highlighter and adding points to help me remember.

◊ Making a mind map from my notes (these help me visualise the topics and understand the connections).

◊ Practice exams (these helped me apply my techniques to an exam situation). After each practice exam I would go over every mistake and copy out the correct answer. Then I taped the answer to the wall of my study. Practice questions are essential to help apply your knowledge.

The busier I've become the more I've had to condense my study time. The following are my tips for getting more out of less time:

◊ Work in 40–50 minute blocks, with a 5–10 minute break after each block.

◊ Set yourself a goal of a number of blocks to get through and stick to it.

◊ Write a list of what you want to get through before you start.

◊ Switch off social media. Spend your break online if you must, but then switch it off when you start your next study block.

◊ Stay away from emails. Emails are my biggest distraction. If I start replying to an email it can completely derail my train of thought.

MANAGE YOUR EXPECTATIONS

Don't be too hard on yourself

Learning to manage your expectations is a significant life hack to managing stress. The more pressure you put on yourself, the more likely it is you will be let down when you can't do everything you want. We're not saying set the bar low; we're saying don't overload your plate. You need to find the balance between challenging yourself and setting realistic goals. You need to have enough energy to give all the things in your life the amount of attention they deserve. Know yourself and listen to the signals your body is sending you. If you're noticing signs that you're under constant stress, then pull back.

LAURA A year ago I thought I could do it all. I tried to manage a university degree, my personal training course and our KIC business. As it turns out, it was too much, and I burnt out very quickly. I was so overwhelmed with my workload that I started to get anxious and was unable to manage any one aspect of it properly. I was overstressed and angry at myself for being so disorganised and unable to live up to my own expectations. I realised I had taken on too much and set myself unachievable goals. I decided to drop down to one subject per semester in my uni degree. This relieved some of the stress but meant I was still working towards my goals.

STEPH Modelling used to stress me out all the time. I would put so much pressure on myself to get each job and be disappointed in myself if I didn't. It was an exhausting rollercoaster of emotions that I just couldn't sustain. So I took the pressure off. I told myself it wasn't possible to get every job. It wasn't that I wasn't beautiful or hard-working enough, there was just someone more suited. These days I tell myself, 'You might not get this, but stay positive'. Then, if I get a job I'm super excited, and if I don't, I'm OK with it.

Managing your expectations can also be applied to your relationships. Again, we're not saying you should lower your standards, but at the same time don't expect the world from everyone around you. It's important to find a balance. You can't control the actions of others and there will be times when someone disappoints you. Remember they're only human and not everyone will see the world the way you do. It's not always fair to expect the people around you to match the expectations you set for yourself.

DON'T SWEAT THE SMALL STUFF

How often do you find yourself getting worked up, anxious and stressed because of something that is out of your control? Here's a simple real-life example; imagine you're in a traffic jam, barely moving, it's been like this for half an hour and there's a car that keeps cutting in and out of the lane in front of you. How does this make you feel? You have two choices. One is to get angry and start honking your horn and yelling at the driver through the window; the other is to take a deep breath and just let it go. The first choice raises your heartbeat, pumps adrenaline through your system and causes all sorts of frustration and bad feelings. The other keeps you calm. You can't control the actions of the other person, so an angry reaction is futile; don't waste your energy. In a short while you'll think back and laugh at the crazy behaviour of the other person.

Always keep in mind that another person's bad behaviour is their responsibility, not yours. Try not to take on their negativity. If you're struggling to stay calm and unaffected, remember that you don't know what it's like to walk in their shoes. You never know what someone else is going through, so choose empathy and walk away.

STEPH I can relate to everyone who finds it hard not to bite back when someone says or does something uncalled for. I have to resist succumbing to the childlike reaction of saying something nasty in return. I found the trolls on Instagram hard to deal with initially because the nasty comments hurt my feelings, but Josh helped me realise that all they wanted was a reaction and they weren't worth my time or energy. Mean words can have a devastating effect, which is why bullies and trolls are rarely brave enough to say horrible things to you in person. They might dish out nastiness and negativity online, but we don't have to take it, let alone believe it. Believe in yourself and the ones you love; try to remember that a faceless name on social media means nothing.

LAURA My favourite way to react to a negative person or a negative situation is to be as kind as possible. Why? Because most people who say something mean or nasty aren't expecting that kind of response. It uses up so much energy when you get angry and emotional, but it's easy to be kind. Most of the time people will be so disarmed by your kindness that they'll apologise and/or realise that what they said or did was completely unwarranted.

TIME TO SWITCH OFF

Secrets of sleep

No matter how healthy your diet is or how much you're exercising, if you don't get enough sleep your body won't feel its best. Sleep is just as important as working out or eating healthily. As adults we need around 7–8 hours a night; however, teenagers need more, around 9–10 hours each night. Some people can function on a little less and some need a bit more. It's vital you work out what's best for you and aim to get that amount every night. Finding the right balance is essential. We often notice when we're not getting enough sleep, but it's also important not to sleep too much. Too much sleep can make us sluggish and lethargic. Try to limit your sleep-ins to one or two a week. We always make sure we get to sleep in at least once a week to let our bodies rest and recuperate.

If you struggle to get to sleep at night, ask yourself why this might be. Are you stressed? Are you looking at a device just before you turn off the light? Is your mind racing?

LAURA I need to sleep at least 8 hours a night to be able to function. I am the most unproductive and grumpy human when I don't get enough sleep! I'll even change my schedule if it's impacting on my sleep. I used to push myself to get up super-early to work out, no matter what time I went to bed; but now I listen to my body and don't push myself too hard. If I'm late to bed because of an event or dinner and I have a huge amount of work the next day, I'll sleep until 8am instead of going to the gym at 6am. If I force myself to get up at 6am to work out, I'll feel tired and grumpy all day and I'll most likely end up craving junk food for the energy boost. I make sleep one of my priorities.

STEPH Like Laura, sleep is extremely important to me. If I haven't had a good sleep, I'm a grump; so, it's best for me and everyone around me that I get my 7-8 hours every night!

We've included the following list of everything we do to help us get to sleep faster at night:

◊ Switch off from work at least two hours before you go to sleep. This lets your mind wind down slowly so it's ready for sleep when your head hits the pillow.

◊ Have a calming tea before bed. We love chamomile or peppermint. Peppermint tea also aids digestion.

◊ Turn your phone onto night mode. It's best not to use your phone before bed, but if you do, have it switched on to night mode. This reduces the brightness of the screen.

◊ Cut out caffeine after midday. Everyone's caffeine tolerance is different, however if you are having trouble sleeping try to make your last coffee before 12 noon, so you can ensure it isn't what is keeping you awake.

◊ Avoid eating chocolate right before bed. This is a tough one, but chocolate contains caffeine so could be contributing to sleep troubles if you're eating it just before you turn in for the night.

7.

Find your

career path

W e would all love that magic combination of a stimulating and fulfilling career that pays well and leaves us plenty of spare time to do the things we love most. But you might not have decided what that career is yet. You might even be struggling to know what subjects to choose at school or uni. And that's fine. Don't feel pressure to know exactly what you want to do at 18 and then do that for the rest of your life. We've learnt that your career will grow with you as you grow — there are lots of options for change once you start university or enter the workforce. But there are also ways to get organised and motivated and be ready to kick the goals when they come your way.

LAURA There's a motto I have always believed in when it comes to school, university and business, which is 'hard work beats talent, when talent doesn't work hard'. I was never particularly book smart at school, so in Year 12 when I set myself the goal of the score I wanted to get, I knew I would have to study my ass off to get there. And I did. The feeling I got from working hard and achieving my goals was amazing. It's addictive. Which is why I'm applying myself just as hard to my law degree. I know I'm not a star student at university, but I'm committed and motivated, so I know I'll get there.

Working hard doesn't just apply to school and your career, it's relevant in all parts of your life. For example, I really wanted a car when I finished high school, but my parents were never able to buy one for me, because they simply couldn't afford it. So I worked two jobs – administration at a hospital by day and waitressing at night – and I saved and saved and bought it myself. I was so proud of that car and I was proud that I'd worked so hard for it. I felt like I could work towards anything! Even today, when something seems too hard or unachievable, I think back to that car and I remember that hard work can get me anywhere I want to be.

If there's one thing I wish I'd been told in high school, it's that there are hundreds of options to choose from when you finish school. University is just one option; there are so many more. The workplace is full of interesting opportunities and many organisations offer rotations and chances to try out different roles which will help you find a job you love. The digital world has opened up so many prospects for young people today that never even existed 10 years ago. For us millennials, the world is our oyster. And remember, you don't need to know exactly what you want to do with your life when you finish school; your work life is a journey, there will be twists and turns and changes, which is exciting and fun. Take your time, chances and opportunities to find what you love, and work hard to make that your career. We spend many hours at work, so it's important to make sure you find something that you enjoy.

The most frequent questions we're asked about our careers are: 'How did you make Keep It Cleaner into the business it is today?' and 'How did you turn your passion into your career?' The answer to the first question can be found in the second. We started Keep It Cleaner to share our easy health tips with others, because that was our passion; we didn't think about it as a means of making money. In fact, we didn't take any money out of the business for quite a long time. Our passion for what we were doing kept us going and turned the venture into something successful. We believe you need passion to be successful in any business. Having passion for what you do means that you're happy to dedicate hours and hours to your business without expecting anything in return. Loving what you do keeps you focused and determined when things go wrong. If you don't love your work, you won't give it 100 per cent. Keep It Cleaner is like our baby: we care about it and want to protect and grow it. If you embark on a career with passion and commitment to work hard, success will come.

We both firmly believe in hard work and passion when it comes to our careers. Growing up in a digital world has made our generation impatient; we're so used to getting instant gratification through all the advances in technology, but when it comes down to it, nothing beats good old hard work.

STEPH I could never have predicted I'd be on the career path I am today. Which is why I want you to know that you don't have to know what you want to do when you finish school. Not everyone knows what they want to study or what they want their lifelong career to be. And many people change their minds. My advice is to work hard to keep your options open. In saying that, I always wanted to be a model. In high school I was told that it was a 'dead end career', and 'not a real job' so I should let it go; but I had to try it. Chasing my dream was the best decision I ever made; if I hadn't followed through I'm sure I wouldn't be the confident woman I am today. I'm also thankful that I kept my options open because I had no idea that modelling would lead me to Keep It Cleaner. When I look at my career today I can see it's a combination of passion and hard work. You can't always know what you want to do, and you can't really know until you go out and do it!

COPING WITH FAILURE

When life teaches you a lesson

This may seem like a strange section for us to include, but like everything else in this book failure is something we have experienced and learnt from. Failure is a crucial part of ongoing success. Through our mistakes we try to learn and grow. We know you will have to make your own mistakes in life, and we have certainly made plenty of our own! Watch other people and learn from their mistakes. Don't go out and make the mistakes they made; go out and make your own!

Our mistakes have been vital to our success; they teach us about ourselves.

Failure and mistakes can take many forms in life. They can feel catastrophically large or insignificantly small. The smallest ones are usually easy to fix; it's the big ones that test our strength. The big mistakes or failures are the ones that teach us the most about ourselves; they make us stronger and more powerful in what we go on to do. Here are a couple of examples of what we're talking about. Firstly, imagine you've chosen a university degree, you've worked hard through school and put all your energy into being accepted into that course, but after the first year you realise it's just not right for you. You're devastated and feel like you've wasted years of your life, and now you're not sure what to do. It's tough, we get it, but look at it this way: by choosing the wrong course you've taken one step closer to finding where your real passion lies. There will be skills that you've learnt in your old course that can be adapted to your next choice and you'll be super motivated to achieve once you find the right path. What felt like a failure has become something positive. In another example, you could find that you launch a new business but it doesn't make any sales. It's a huge blow because you believed in what you were doing. But look at it this way: you now know more about what doesn't work. So use your disappointment and all the time and money you invested as motivation to make the next business work better. You've got the experience under your hat now, so you can use it to push forward. Don't be scared of starting a job and not loving it as much as you had hoped either – it means you are one step closer to finding something you do love.

Mistakes are a part of life; don't fear them. At the end of the day, remember you always learn more when you give something a go than if you never try at all. The one rule we both live by is to not make the same mistake twice. Learn from what you did wrong and move on.

STEPH I learnt from my end of school exams that you need to be your own motivation. More often than not I would wait for my mum to tell me to go and study, rather than taking the initiative for myself. I was lucky that I wasn't in need of an amazing score to do what I wanted to do after school, but I used that as an excuse in school to not give it my all. One particular regret I have is that I didn't prepare for the exam in my favourite subject. Throughout Year 12, I was getting As in Studio Arts and I took for granted that I would ace the exam, so didn't schedule any time to study. I thought I'd be fine. I walked out of that exam knowing that I hadn't done enough and was likely to get a really poor mark. It was the worst feeling ever. I walked home crying. What this showed me however, was that my success was my responsibility. I learnt from this experience that you can never be too well prepared.

GOAL SETTING

Ready, set, goal

Setting goals is something everyone talks about. Many of us make an attempt to write them down. But few of us remember to go back and look at what we've written and make a conscious effort to achieve them. One of the biggest mistakes we, and many others, have made is to set ambitious goals without a clear idea of how we should go about achieving them. We can feel super-motivated about our goals, but unless we've thought through the pathway to achieving them we're setting ourselves up for failure. We think the best way to get to where you want to go is to set smaller, attainable goals that can be ticked off along the way.

For example, you might want to buy a car. Instead of just writing down that you want a car, work out how much money you'll need to save and what work you'll need to do to make the money. Set the small goals, such as: writing a resume, dropping resumes off, applying online etc. Once you get a job, work out how much of your income you need to save to achieve the big goal of buying the car. In setting these smaller, achievable goals you're more likely to stay on track to reach the main goal.

You can set goals for anything and everything you like! Just make sure they are realistic and set them out in detail, so you stay accountable and on track to making them happen.

YOUR GOALS

Use this space below to write out your goals.
Remember to include the smaller goals you need
to achieve before you can reach your end goal.

8.
Exercise

*P*ushing your body to move every day is one of the best things you can do for yourself. In fact, our bodies are wired to reward us for exercise. When we work out, pushing our heart rate up, our brain releases chemicals known as endorphins, which make us feel good.

Exercise also does great things to our bodies that aren't always as obvious as the initial endorphin rush. Regular exercise helps us fight off health problems like high blood pressure and heart disease. It keeps our bones strong and boosts our energy levels by making our cardiovascular system work hard, which improves the way our heart and lungs work. And it helps us sleep better too. What's not to love?

We think this chapter is one of the most important in the book. Not just because of how good exercise makes you feel, but also because we know that working out can be hard and can sometimes feel unachievable. We want you to feel as inspired as we do, and we believe if you get your head into the right mindset and establish a solid routine, you won't go back.

LAURA I used to work out solely for my physical appearance. I was obsessed with spending hours in the gym every day. I was so focused on the calories I was burning that I didn't allow myself to enjoy my workout. I had images of very thin models on my phone that I would use to try to motivate myself. I fixated on having a 'thigh gap' and would work out every day, becoming unreasonably frustrated if something upset my routine. And for what? My body isn't genetically designed to have a thigh gap, so no matter how hard I tried I wasn't going to achieve it. I was working towards something unattainable and making myself miserable in the process. I decided to take a step back and reassess my reasons for working out. I could see that the mindset I was in was a toxic one, full of negative influences. I decided to look at my workouts a different way, I started to work out for the way it made me feel not for how it made me look. I now make time to listen to my body, which is SO IMPORTANT. If I wake up and feel tired or run down, then I have a rest day, or I swap a high intensity workout for a gentle walk outside. I used to feel guilty if I took a day off when I was tired, but now I don't feel any guilt for listening to what my body is trying to tell me. Remember to tell yourself: one workout won't make you fit, just as skipping one workout won't make you unfit!

STEPH When I went through my period of poor eating I was also destroying myself in the gym. I was angry at myself for what I'd eaten and would work out morning and night, pushing myself to tears, or to the point of injury. I was so unhappy, and working out for all the wrong reasons. I had negative thoughts going through my head constantly and I was in a vicious cycle of guilt and punishment. I wasn't in control of my reasons for exercising so I couldn't get any pleasure from my workouts. I needed to shift my mindset and take control.

POSITIVE MINDSET

Why do we work out?

One of the most common reasons to drop out of an exercise routine is that you have come to the end of a challenge over a particular time frame, or you participated in an event you were working towards. It's easy to give up in these circumstances because your motivation has run its course. To help maintain your motivation, sit down and write what you feel after you work out. Try to concentrate on the way you are feeling, not your appearance. The secret to making exercise part of your routine for life is not about how it makes you look; it's about how moving your body makes you FEEL.

Do you feel happy, strong, empowered and confident after a workout? It will be different for everyone, but it is SO important to think about how it makes you feel. We believe you are less likely to skip workouts if you're aware of all the positive feelings you will miss if you upset your routine.

STEPH My mindset shifted when I started concentrating on what made me happy. I relaxed my focus on food and stopped stressing about how I was eating. I started going to the gym with a more positive attitude: I went to build strength, get fit and feel energised. Exercise stopped being a punishment and became something that made me happy and healthy. It's now as much a part of my routine as brushing my teeth. It's the first thing I do six days of the week.

LAURA I have always struggled to set aside 'me time'. So my promise to myself every day is to get my workout done, which means 30-60 minutes of time just for me. Every day is different, but the energy and mental clarity I get from my workout is a constant. If I skip my workout, I know I will have less energy, I'll feel lethargic and I'll start the day more stressed. I see my workout as the battery recharge for my brain each day. I do a lot of my planning and goal setting while I'm running and it always helps me destress. I find that no matter how big a problem is, or how complex a stressful situation might be, it always seems easier to tackle when I've finished my run.

ESTABLISHING
YOUR ROUTINE

Our tips to keep on track

The key to staying active is routine. Once you have established a good routine, it's easy. The hard part is starting and setting the routine. We promise you that once you set your routine, it will be SO much easier to stay motivated every day. Trust us and push through the first few difficult weeks of your new life.

No matter how fit you currently are, once were, or have never been, it starts the same way. Focus on the fact that when you look back a month from now, you will have made a month's progress. Starting is the hardest part. This is the start of the journey towards being the healthiest and happiest version of yourself you can be. You will not regret it, you will only wish you had started sooner! If you are waiting for a sign to start, THIS IS IT. Do it for YOU.

OUR TIPS FOR GETTING STARTED

Write down in your diary all your workouts at the start of every week.

With your workout in writing it's harder to ignore. Ticking off your workout each day will also give you a sense of achievement and keep you accountable to yourself.

LOOK AT YOUR WORKOUTS AS APPOINTMENTS

You would never cancel an appointment that inconvenienced somebody else, so why do it to yourself? Make your workout a non-negotiable appointment. Show yourself the same respect you would show a friend, work colleague or client. If you must cancel, reschedule it, just like any other meeting.

DON'T EXPECT TO FEEL THE SAME ABOUT EVERY WORKOUT

We don't wake up every day with the same motivation to work out. If we only worked out when we felt motivated, we would perhaps exercise one day in five! Sometimes our motivation takes a while to kick in, but power through and we promise it will kick in once you get going.

PUT YOUR CLOTHES OUT THE NIGHT BEFORE

The less you have to think about in the morning, the better.

WORK OUT WITH A FRIEND

Working out with a friend makes you accountable, and it's fun. If you don't have a workout mate, we have created our online program so you can have us as your workout buddies! The Keep It Cleaner community is strong and encouraging and you'll find no end of motivation once you're involved.

PLAN YOUR WORKOUTS

Plan which workout you're going to do beforehand so that you can step straight into it. Detail the different workouts as part of your diary entry at the start of the week. Before we developed our own program, we often wasted time at the gym trying to decide what to do. Having a planned workout keeps you focused and results in a good session.

An effective workout doesn't mean spending hours in the gym each day. And if you think slaving away on the treadmill is the only way to get active, we've got good news. There are SO many more exciting ways to move your body. We want you to enjoy your exercise so here are our favourite workouts.

MOVE YOUR BODY

Our favourite forms of exercise

BOXING

STEPH Boxing is one of my absolute favourite ways to work up a sweat, and boy do I SWEAT! There's nothing quite like it. For me, boxing is like therapy. If I'm upset or annoyed about something, I tend to have an even better session because I punch harder and faster and I'm driven to not give up.

You don't need a boxing gym to box, you don't even need a boxing bag! Just grab some gloves and a pair of pads and workout with a mate! Or if you're working out on your own, work on your skipping and shadow boxing skills! Shadow boxing might look easy, but it's a great way to get your heart rate going without equipment and is also a great way to work on your technique.

LAURA I love boxing because it's a whole-body workout and a great way to relieve stress. You can literally punch away your stress. Boxing is great for toning your arms and strengthening your core, and I love that you can incorporate it into all your workouts through skipping or shadow boxing. To anyone who doubts their coordination skills and feels intimidated by boxing – don't worry, I felt the same but found I could give it a go. So you can do it too!

HIIT

High Intensity Interval Training (HIIT) is an all-in, fast-paced workout that will leave you out of breath and totally invigorated. HIIT involves quick bursts of intense exercise, followed by short recovery periods or low intensity exercise. It gets your heart rate up quickly and keeps it up for longer. We love it.

STEPH The best thing about HIIT is you can do it anywhere and you only need to work out for a short amount of time. In other words, it's super-efficient. The other amazing thing about HIIT is that it boosts your metabolism for up to 24 hours after you finish exercising. Which means you continue to burn calories even once you've finished your workout. Don't stress if you don't have any equipment at home, or you don't have a gym to go to. HIIT workouts can be done with bodyweight only, no equipment necessary.

LAURA This is my FAVOURITE way to get my heart rate up. HIIT is a great form of cardio for anyone who doesn't like cardio, and you can do it anywhere at any time. I love combining a HIIT running/floor workout and do at least two of these sessions per week.

STRENGTH TRAINING

Strength training isn't just about building lean muscle and muscle definition; it is about much more than how it makes you look on the outside. Strength training makes you stronger. That sounds obvious, we know, but don't underestimate how good it feels to be strong. Strength training also protects your bones, helps your coordination and improves your posture and your balance.

STEPH My favourite type of strength training is bodyweight and light resistance strength training. For example, pilates-based strength training. Pilates is incredible for your all-round body strength, posture and balance. The exercises strengthen your core to a whole other level. My posture has improved so much since strengthening my core. You don't need a reformer bed to do Pilates-based strength training either; you just need a floor and a workout routine to follow. The strength workouts in our program are both body resistance exercises and weight training.

And before you start worrying that weight training might make you bulky, stop! Weight training can burn as much fat as a solid cardio session. How? Well, strength training increases lean muscle mass, and the more lean muscle mass you hold, the easier it is to burn calories. Also, who wouldn't want to feel strong and powerful?

LAURA Feeling strong is awesome. I do strength training because I love to feel strong and be confident that I can do things for myself. Even the seemingly small task of carrying all the grocery bags inside at once, instead of making two trips, makes me feel proud! Strength training doesn't just mean lifting heavy weights in the gym, it can be as basic as adding push-ups or squats to your sessions. And if you want to add some extra resistance and you don't have access to a gym or weights, you can use anything you have around the house. Rice bags, full water bottles and even small children work a treat.

RUNNING

LAURA Anyone who follows me on social media might assume I have always been a runner, and a good runner at that. However, the truth is I haven't always been good at it. My younger sister, Sienna, has always been an amazing runner, and I always wished I could run like her. She won countless cross-country meets and competed at state level every year. I used to think I could never be as good as her because I wasn't a 'natural' runner and I never did well in my cross-country races at school. I had a light bulb moment during Year 10, when I realised the only reason I didn't want to run was because I was telling myself I couldn't be a runner. I decided to start training and working hard and that year I placed for the first time in my life at my high school cross-country. I proved to myself that it wasn't always about natural talent but it was also about hard work. We often decide too early that we're not good at something because we don't excel at the first attempt, so if you have always thought that running was not for you, ask yourself why. Chances are you can do it.

Now that I'm in my twenties, running is my favourite way to move my body. I start to feel crazy if I go for longer than a week without running. I love to mix it up with long endurance runs and interval training (short bursts of energy followed by rest). My favourite thing about running is that you can do it anywhere at any time; all you need is a good pair of shoes. It is an important stress reliever for me and I love how empowered and strong I feel when I get back from a long run or tough interval session. My advice to anyone who wants to start running is to just do it! And remember that everyone starts somewhere. Set small goals to begin, get a great playlist, and get going.

STEPH I have a love-hate relationship with running. It has never been my favourite form of exercise and it probably never will be. But that doesn't mean I give up on it. Recently, Laura has motivated me to keep up with my running training, and, slowly but surely, I have improved. I don't hate it as much as I used to because I've fallen in love with the feeling I get when I finish a run. I've also become competitive with myself. I WANT to improve at it, so I WILL.

Our favourite workout plans

We love to mix up our workouts to keep them fun and exciting and to stop us getting bored. We have included an example of one of the seven-day workouts from our online program that you can do anywhere, at any time. You don't need a gym to work out, you just need to be creative (although you will need a skipping rope for the Boxing workout). Our workouts are different every day, because we always want to challenge our bodies. Just as it's important to have variety in your diet, it's important to have variations in your workouts too. To get the most out of our workouts, you need to challenge yourself! The harder you work, the fitter you will get and the more accomplished you will feel at the end of your workout.

NOTE: The workouts we've included here are all filmed as part of our online program, so let us be your workout buddies!

> **If you don't have weights on hand, here are some alternatives:**
>
> ◊   Bags of rice
> ◊   Full water bottles
> ◊   Cans of beans
> ◊   A whole watermelon

GLOSSARY OF OUR WORKOUT TERMS

BURPEES
Start in a standing position, squat down and place your hands on the ground, shoulder-width apart. Now jump your feet back and extend your legs so you land in a plank position. Jump your feet back to your hands and jump up to standing again.

CROSS PUNCH
Stand with one foot slightly forward of the other with your knees slightly bent. A cross punch is a forward movement where you're extending your arm right out in front of you, twisting your upper body forward so that your shoulder follows through.

DUMBBELL-WEIGHTED SQUATS
Hold two dumbbells at chest height as you squat – hips back, knees out, with feet pointed at 45 degrees. Keep your weight through your heels.

GRAVEYARDS
Start in a plank position on your hands, come down onto your forearms holding the plank position and back up to a plank position on your hands. Your feet should be shoulder-width apart (though for more of a challenge have your feet closer together).

HALF BURPEES
Place your hands on the ground just in front of your feet, then jump your feet back and extend your legs to plank position. Jump your feet back to your hands and repeat. This is the same movement as a regular burpee (above) except that you're not coming up to standing position at all.

HEEL TOUCHES
Lie down on your back with your knees raised and your feet flat on the ground, close to your bottom, shoulder-width apart. Lift your shoulders off the ground so that you're in a crunch position, with your arms extended along your sides. Stretch one hand at a time to the same side heel and tap. Keep your shoulders off the ground.

HOOK PUNCH

Stand with one foot slightly forward of the other with your knees slightly bent. A hook punch is when you punch forward across your body, with your elbow held high.

JAB PUNCH

Stand with one foot slightly forward of the other with your knees slightly bent. A jab punch is where you punch out with the arm of your leading shoulder, extending it right in front of you.

LATERAL HOPS

Start on one leg, hopping laterally as far as possible, then land on the other foot and repeat. Aim to keep one foot off the ground at all times.

LEG RAISES

Lie down on your back and place your hands underneath your bottom to support your lower back. Straighten your legs and then roll your hips towards your chest to raise your legs up to the sky. Slowly bring them back down to the ground, controlling them with your core. Bring your legs back up and repeat. Make sure your lower back doesn't lift off the floor.

MOUNTAIN CLIMBERS

In a plank position on your hands, bring one knee to your elbow. Keep your back straight and your core engaged the whole time. Repeat with the other leg.

PLANK

From lying, face down, with your hands or forearms shoulder-width apart, lift your body straight and level off the ground and hold. Keep your legs extended and your toes on the ground. Keep your core engaged and don't let your hips or lower back dip down. Ankles, knees, hips and shoulders should be aligned.

PLANK WITH FORWARD REACH

Holding the plank position, reach one arm forwards and tap the ground in front of you. Keep your back straight and your core engaged the whole time. Repeat with the other arm. Move your feet wider apart to make the exercise easier, or closer together to make it more difficult.

PLANK SHOULDER TAPS

Holding the plank position, use one hand to tap the opposite shoulder. Keep your back straight and your core engaged the whole time. Repeat with the other hand.

POWER UPPERS

This is the same as an 'upper' (see next page) but put more power and force into each punch.

REVERSE BURPEES

Start in a standing position and squat down until your bottom hits the floor. Rock backwards and bring your knees to your chest, building up enough momentum to rock back up onto your feet and jump up to finish.

REVERSE CRUNCH

Start by lying on your back with your knees bent and your feet on the floor in front of your hips. Have your arms/hands by your side with palms facing the ground. Engage your core and bring both knees to your chest, lifting your bottom slightly off the ground. Bring your feet back down to tap the floor, then repeat.

REVERSE LUNGES

Step backwards with one leg. Bend both legs 90 degrees so that your back knee is almost touching the ground and your front knee isn't tracking over your toes. Bring that leg back to standing position and repeat with the other leg. Make sure you finish with your hips soft and your glutes engaged.

RUSSIAN TWISTS

From a sitting position on the floor, form your body into a 'V' shape. Have your legs bent in front of you and lean back, keeping your lower back straight, with your pelvis tucked back and your core engaged. Twist your upper body from side to side, rotating through your torso. Elevate your feet off the floor and hold your bent legs at a 90 degree angle for a more advanced option.

SIDE PLANK

Start on your side with your feet together and your forearm (or hand) directly below your shoulder. Engage your core and lift your hips up until your body is in a straight line from your head to your toes.

SPRINTER SIT-UPS

Lying flat on your back with your legs extended, bring one knee to your chest as you crunch up and lift your shoulders off the floor to end up in a frozen running position. Keep your other leg flat on the ground. Slowly lower your leg and shoulders back to the ground and repeat on the other side.

SQUAT JUMPS

Come down into a squat position and jump in the air as high as you can. Land softly on your feet and then back down into a squat position.

SQUAT PULSES

From a squat position, pulse between a deep squat and halfway to standing.

STEP-UPS

Find a box or a stair and step up on one leg until it's straight. Step lightly back and repeat with the other leg.

TOE TOUCHES

Laying on your back, extend your legs straight up to the sky, so that your body makes the shape of an 'L'. Lift your shoulders off the ground and crunch up reaching for your toes.

UPPER

Stand with one foot slightly forward of the other with your knees slightly bent. Dip your shoulder down as you make a fist and punch upwards in a scoop motion.

WALL SIT

With your feet shoulder-width apart, squat with your back against a wall. Keep your legs bent in front of you and the weight through your heels.

Day 1

HIIT

This high-intensity workout will leave you out of breath and covered in sweat, but full of energy for the day. This one is packed with the fun stuff, including burpees (learn to love them!), skipping, high knees running and more. Use the stopwatch on your phone to time each round.

Duration: 30 minutes

Round 1

Allow a 30-second rest between each round

30 seconds x burpees
30 seconds x plank
Repeat x 5

Round 2

45 seconds x high knees running
15 seconds rest

45 seconds x skipping
15 seconds rest

45 seconds x high knees running
15 seconds rest

45 seconds x skipping
15 seconds rest

45 seconds x high knees running
15 seconds rest

Round 3

As many reps as possible (AMRAP) in 5 minutes

10 x squats
5 x push-ups
5 x burpees

Round 4

10 x burpees
1 x push-up

9 x burpees
2 x push-ups

8 x burpees
3 x push-ups

And so on, until you get to 1 x burpee, 10 x push-ups

Day 2

RUNNING

For anyone who thinks running is boring, this one is for you! The resting and running combo keeps it interesting. All you need is a motivating playlist and a safe place to run. You can do this workout on a treadmill, at the park, or on a running track.

Duration: 30 mins

Intervals

5-minute jog (or brisk walk) to warm up

30-second run x 30-second break
(repeat 20 times)

5-minute jog (or walk) to cool down

Day 3

BOXING

Time to punch it out! You can use small dumbbells during the boxing rounds for an extra challenge and make sure you brace your core throughout to ensure you train your abdominals as well as your arms.

Duration: 20 minutes

Round 1

45 seconds x skipping
15 seconds rest

45 seconds x sit-ups + 1-2 punch (if you haven't boxed before, a 1-2 punch is just a quick punch from both left and right)
15 seconds rest

45 seconds x heel touches
15 seconds rest

45 seconds x skipping
15 seconds rest

45 seconds x plank
15 seconds rest

Round 2

45 seconds x jab cross
15 seconds rest

45 seconds x jab cross
hook cross
15 seconds rest

45 seconds x weighted
power uppers
15 seconds rest

45 seconds x jab cross
upper left, upper right
15 seconds rest

45 seconds x kneeling
weighted hooks
15 seconds rest

Round 3

45 seconds x Russian twists
with punch
15 seconds rest

45 seconds x leg raises
15 seconds rest

45 seconds x toe touches
15 seconds rest

45 seconds x sit-up double
arm punch
15 seconds rest

45 seconds x heel touches
15 seconds rest

Round 4

45 seconds x skipping
15 seconds rest

45 seconds x plank
15 seconds rest

45 seconds x skipping
15 seconds rest

45 seconds x plank
15 seconds rest

45 seconds x skipping
15 seconds rest

Day 4

STRENGTH

Time to strengthen those muscles. You can add a weight to any of the lunges, squats, Russian twists, squat holds and step ups. It's completely up to you. Though keep in mind, we want you to CHALLENGE YOURSELF.

Duration: 20 minutes

Round 1

45 seconds x push-ups
15 seconds rest

45 seconds x plank shoulder taps
15 seconds rest

45 seconds X reverse crunches
15 seconds rest

45 seconds x graveyards
15 seconds rest

45 seconds x plank with forward reach
15 seconds rest

Round 2

45 seconds x squat pulses
15 seconds rest

45 seconds x reverse lunges
15 seconds rest

45 seconds x dumbbell-weighted squats
15 seconds rest

45 seconds x step-ups
15 seconds rest

45 seconds x wall sit or squat hold
15 seconds rest

Round 3

Russian twists alternating with mountain climbers
15 seconds on and 15 seconds rest for 5 minutes

Round 4

Plank and squat challenge: Hold a plank for as long as you can up to 5 minutes. When you stop, hold a squat for 5 minutes.

Day 5

HIIT

Another killer HIIT workout! This one works your whole body. We've added an extra round as a challenge. Aim for four rounds, but if you have some extra energy, push for five.

Duration: 25 minutes

Round 1

15 seconds on, 15 seconds off high knees x 10

Round 2

45 seconds x sprinter sit-ups
15 seconds rest

45 seconds x lateral hops
15 seconds rest

45 seconds x sit-ups
15 seconds rest

45 seconds x squat jumps
15 seconds rest

45 seconds x sprinter sit-ups
15 seconds rest

Round 3

Half burpees alternating with graveyards
15 seconds on and
15 seconds rest

Round 4

AMRAP in 5 mins
10 toe touches
10 heel touches
10 reverse burpees

Round 5

45 seconds x star jumps
15 seconds rest

45 seconds x plank
15 seconds rest

45 seconds x side plank
15 seconds rest

45 seconds x side plank
15 seconds rest

45 seconds X burpees
15 seconds rest

Day 6

BOXING

Time to work on your boxing again. The more practice you get, the less silly you'll feel doing the shadow boxing. It won't be long until you're a boxing machine!

Duration: 20 minutes

Round 1

15 seconds x jab cross and 15 seconds rest x 10

Round 2

45 seconds x skipping
15 seconds rest

45 seconds x kneeling weighted hooks
15 seconds rest

45 seconds x skipping
15 seconds rest

45 seconds x jab cross
15 seconds rest

45 seconds x skipping
15 seconds rest

Round 3

AMRAP in 5 mins
10 x jab cross
10 x sit-ups
10 x burpees

Round 4

45 seconds x skipping
15 seconds rest

45 seconds x plank
15 seconds rest

45 seconds x side plank
15 seconds rest

45 seconds x (opposite) side plank
15 seconds rest

45 seconds x skipping
15 seconds rest

Day 7

RUNNING

It's time for your endurance run. Choose a level that works for you. When it comes to running it's essential that you start with an achievable distance for your fitness level, to avoid any injuries. Our rule is to increase the distance you run by 10 per cent each week, to build up gradually.

If you are brand new to running, try to run for the duration of one song, then walk for the next song, until you can build up to running nonstop.

Beginner

Run 2 km (one song on and one off, or jog the whole time)

Intermediate

Run 5 km (try to do this without stopping)

Advanced

Run 8 km (no stopping)

9.
You are what
you eat

When it comes to healthy eating we like to keep it simple. There are so many fad diets that promote a particular way of eating as the best for maintaining a healthy lifestyle or the best way for losing weight. But we believe that the key to having a healthy relationship with food is to adopt the practice of mindful eating. No tricks or shortcuts or skipping meals — mindful eating is about understanding what you're eating and why you're eating it. A mindful eater fuels their body with all the right nutrients so it can function to the best of its ability. This largely means eating fresh and unprocessed, unpackaged foods, but it does allow for treats, just in quantities that make sense for healthy living. It's about enjoying what you eat and eating what makes you feel good, inside and out.

DIETS

A plan for healthy eating

While we don't stick to any specific diet, we wanted to run through some of the more popular eating plans and diets that we see people following today. Of course, we are not trained nutritionists – this is all just interesting information we've picked up along the way. So please make sure to get advice before you suddenly change your diet.

CALORIE COUNTING

Calories are essentially units of energy. The number of calories a food contains is about the amount of energy that food provides. To maintain a healthy weight, it's important that your calorie intake doesn't exceed the number of calories your body burns each day. This is where the calorie counting comes in. The right number of calories for your body depends on how much physical activity you do and your metabolism; there isn't a magic number that works for everybody. You need to be able to track your activity alongside your calorie intake to ensure a balance. For some people, the simple yet scientific nature of the calorie-controlled diet provides an easy to understand cause and effect structure around an eating plan. Calorie counting hasn't worked for us in the past – not because the science doesn't work, more because of the anxiety that counting calories caused us. We found the focus on calories made us forget to look at food for its nutritional benefits. There may be the same number of calories in a couple of squares of chocolate as there is in a bowl of broccoli, but the broccoli is so much better for your body. As a basic way of maintaining a certain weight, calorie counting is effective - just choose what's right for you.

STEPH Calorie counting doesn't work for me. I have tried it a few times and only lasted a few days each time. The problem for me was that I became far too rigid about the number of calories I allocated myself each day and I would get upset and angry if I went over the limit. It wasn't the kind of relationship I wanted to have with food, but it did help me understand that I wanted to look at food as fuel source and not a number. It led me to a more mindful way of eating.

LAURA Calorie counting caused me a great deal of anxiety around food. I found that tracking calories would lead me to skip meals or cancel on dinner plans when I couldn't be sure of the calorie content in the food. I used an online app to add up my daily intake and I became obsessed with entering in every little detail. I stopped enjoying food and I stopped thinking about the benefits of the food I was eating. I became addicted to calorie-free foods like sugar-free soft drinks, and highly processed sugar-free foods that were made up of chemicals that were terrible for my body.

VEGETARIANISM & VEGANISM

Most people choose to be vegetarian or vegan on environmental or ethical grounds. They don't believe that humans should eat meat (or too much meat), and vegans also avoid any products that are derived from animals. Some people also make the choice to avoid eating animals and animal products because they don't like the way it tastes or makes them feel; or they may have an intolerance that prevents them from enjoying meat, eggs, honey or dairy. Neither of us are vegan or vegetarian, but we totally respect the choices of people who are. We respect people's personal beliefs and we respect anyone who listens to their body and does what's right for them. One important thing to remember when choosing a lifestyle like veganism or vegetarianism is that in eliminating an entire food group from your diet you may also eliminate an essential source of nutrition. You need to be conscious of adding the missing nutrition into your diet via another source. For example, red meat is a great source of iron which helps red blood cells transport oxygen throughout our bodies; without iron we become anaemic, so we need to make sure we're including an iron-rich substitute like wholegrain bread and cereals, nuts and seeds, or lots of leafy greens.

LAURA I struggle with low energy levels when I don't eat meat. If this is the same for you, but you want to make some ethical decisions about where your food (particularly the meat) comes from, here are a few tips:

◊   Always buy free-range eggs.

◊   Buy free-range chicken and other meats that have been ethically sourced (look for the free-range standards-approved sticker if you're buying from the supermarket).

◊   Support your local farmers: shop at local farmers' markets whenever you can or look for products that you know are local.

◊   Eat seasonal produce (eating produce out of season either racks up air miles or means it has been grown in an energy-guzzling hothouse).

◊   Avoid fast food (almost all the fast food restaurants use produce that has been raised on factory farms; and they also use far too much packaging, hence rubbish).

◊   Have a meat-free day each week to help reduce our overall meat consumption.

OMELETTE THREE WAYS, PAGE 170

STEPH I have experimented with veganism and being vegetarian for health reasons and I struggled with it. My blood type processes red meat well and it's an excellent source of iron for me. It's a food I crave, and I feel good when it's in my diet. Saying that, I don't eat it every day. I've found a balance that works best for me. I eat a great deal of vegan and vegetarian food, I just don't label what I'm eating. I'm eating what I know my body needs.

GLUTEN FREE

Gluten-free diets are for those people who are allergic to gluten or have a gluten intolerance or sensitivity. Gluten IS NOT bad for everyone, and food labelled as 'gluten free' doesn't necessarily mean it's 'healthy'. If you have an intolerance, allergy or sensitivity – which means your system can't handle the gluten found in wheat, barley and rye – then you need a gluten-free diet. For everyone else, going gluten-free is unnecessary. Just remember to always read the ingredients of the products you are buying, as sometimes they can be overly processed and not necessarily healthy. We are both gluten intolerant (not allergic), so we avoid gluten when we can, but we still eat it sometimes.

SUGAR FREE

There are different versions of the sugar-free diet around but it's essentially about cutting out ALL sugar from your diet and then gradually introducing a small amount of natural sugar (fresh fruit, honey etc) back in. Eating a diet high in refined sugar, including soft drinks, confectionery and other processed sugary food, isn't great for anyone's health. Our bodies aren't designed to process lots of refined sugars so eating too much will inevitably cause weight gain and all the associated risks that go along with being overweight.

STEPH I don't follow a sugar-free diet, but I do keep my refined sugar to a minimum. Healthy sugars, like fruit, on the other hand I can't get enough of! There isn't a day that goes by when I don't have a piece of fruit.

LAURA I believe in 'everything in moderation' and while I don't drink soft drinks, I do indulge my chocolate or lolly craving every now and then. Refined sugar is an occasional food for me. And, like Steph, I can't live without fruit! I have it every day and it's packed with so much delicious goodness that I could never completely cut it out.

We find that if we eat fats as part of a meal, it not only keeps us satisfied and our sugar cravings at bay, but it also helps our minds to stay focused.

FAT FREE

There was once the belief that following a diet containing no fats meant you wouldn't get fat. But it doesn't work like that. There are fats you should avoid and others that make up part of a healthy, balanced diet. Monounsaturated and polyunsaturated are the healthy fats found in nuts, seeds, olive oil, peanut oil, avocados, egg yolk and fish. These fats are good for our cholesterol, which in the long run helps our hearts. The fats to watch out for are saturated fats and trans-fats. Saturated fats, like those found in cheese and some meats, are fine in moderation but will raise cholesterol levels if eaten too much. Trans-fats are those found in highly processed foods like margarine, potato chips, biscuits, crackers, donuts, cake mix and fried fast food. There are absolutely no nutritional benefits to eating trans-fats and there are many drawbacks, not least being they increase your chances of heart disease and stroke. As with all packaged products, we recommend you check all the ingredients, as sometimes fats are replaced with sugar or processed nasties.

STEPH I love cooking with butter and olive oil, and I love cheese! So, a fat-free diet has never been on my radar. But I do try to stay aware of the good fats vs the bad fats!

LAURA My diet is full of healthy fats. The fats that come from avocado, olive oil and nuts are extremely good for us. I find that when I add a healthy fat to my meal I'm full for longer and not craving snacks an hour after I've eaten.

THE 80:20 RULE

The idea of the 80:20 rule is to eat as healthily as you can for 80 per cent of the time and treat yourself to the foods you love for the other 20 per cent of the time. When you allow yourself some treat foods, you're less likely to succumb to binge eating, which can happen if your diet is too strict.

STEPH This eating plan is a great way for me to stay on track (on holidays it may be more like 70:30, because: holidays). If I'm too strict on myself and cut out foods that I love, I end up binging on them as soon as I have the chance, which is not a healthy or positive mindset for me.

LAURA I'm a big fan of the 80:20 principle. I interpret it as eating well the majority of the time and treating myself every now and then. It's about nourishing my body but not depriving myself. You don't need to measure out your foods exactly; it's just about keeping the principle in mind. I usually have one or two 'naughty' meals a week and eat healthy for the rest of the time. (Though some weeks I might not have any 'naughty' meals and other weeks I might have four!) I don't worry about being too strict because I know I'm healthy most of the time!

THE FOOD PRINCIPLES

Guiding our healthy living

In this section we want to share with you everything we have learned about food and how it relates to our healthy living. We hope that you can take away a few tips to help create a healthier diet for yourself and that you see our tips and suggestions as practical and sustainable long-term solutions to a healthier lifestyle. Our secret to living a healthy lifestyle isn't a quick fix or fad diet, it's a series of simple and easy changes. As you'll see in this section, healthy isn't complicated, anyone can do it, you just need to trust us and trust in yourself.

EAT WHOLE FOODS

Whole foods are as simple as they sound. They are foods that haven't been processed or refined and are purchased in their natural state. Examples of whole foods are fresh vegetables, fruit, eggs, meat (without additives), nuts, natural yoghurt, raw milk, whole grains, legumes, fish and shellfish (without additives), etc. Whole foods should form the base of your diet and make up a majority of what you eat.

EAT FAT

Healthy fats of course! As we touched on earlier, healthy fats are good for you and are an essential part of a healthy and a balanced diet. Healthy fats help to keep you feeling full, so we make sure we include a source of good fat in every meal. We believe the healthy fats in our diet keep us satisfied and keep our sugar cravings at bay, as well as keeping our minds focused. Healthy fats also contribute to vibrant, glowing skin and shiny healthy hair. Our favourite forms of healthy fat are avocados, extra virgin olive oil (EVOO), salmon, eggs, nuts and full-fat natural yoghurt. And remember, just like everything else, eat healthy fat in moderation.

EVERYTHING IN MODERATION

We believe that a diet full of variety is what makes us feel our best. We're not about completely cutting out a food group – instead, we believe in eating in moderation. This goes for sweets and 'treat' foods too. In our experience when we cut out everything 'naughty' and try to eat clean 100 per cent of the time, we end up giving in and bingeing because we have deprived ourselves. If we have a craving for some dark chocolate after dinner, we have some! But instead of having an entire block we have a couple of squares instead. Remember that one unhealthy meal won't make you unhealthy, just like one healthy meal won't make you healthy. It's OK to have a couple of meals a week that aren't healthy; just make sure the other meals are healthy and full of whole foods.

LOOK AFTER YOUR GUT HEALTH

You might have heard the words 'gut health' used a lot these days when talking about general well-being, and for good reason! Having a healthy gut is fundamental to feeling your best and having a strong immune system. A healthy gut prevents inflammation and bloating and makes sure our digestive system is working at its best. It even helps you sleep better at night. We want to have an abundance of healthy bacteria in our gut always, which you will do if you follow a healthy, balanced diet rich in whole foods! There are also some special healthy-bacteria-packed foods containing pre- and probiotics that can help boost our gut health. These foods include kombucha, fermented vegetables such as sauerkraut and kimchi, kefir, natural yoghurt and apple cider vinegar. It is especially important to focus on eating an abundance of good bacteria when we have taken a course of antibiotics. This is because antibiotics kill bacteria, both good and bad, which means we need to help our bodies build the healthy bacteria back up again.

Stress and eating lots of junk food (processed food) are also bad for our healthy gut bacteria. So if you've been experiencing stress it could be worth taking a probiotic to counteract the effect on your gut. Try to keep processed food to a minimum and make room for your 'me time' each day.

We believe that a diet full of variety is what makes us feel our best.

LIMIT PROCESSED FOODS

Processed foods are foods that are not in their natural state. We don't believe it's feasible to completely cut out all processed foods; however, we do think it's important to limit them as much as you can. We know it's not always possible to make the pasta sauce from scratch or cook up a stock for a couple of hours! You need to make your healthy lifestyle achievable and sustainable. All credit to those people who eat 100 per cent organic and ethically sourced food all the time. Many of us, however, struggle to achieve this level of healthy eating. We also don't want a healthy lifestyle to be a difficult one. We love cooking our meals from scratch, but we don't always have the time, so we sometimes buy pre-made. With this said, there are a few basic rules we stick to when buying anything processed.

When you pick up a processed item, turn it around and read the ingredients list and the nutritional information on the back of the packet. Check the ingredients. Our rule of thumb is, the fewer ingredients the better, and if there are any words that sound like laboratory chemicals, we don't buy

the product. The ingredients are listed in order of their percentage make-up, so the first ingredient is what makes up most of the product. So if that is 'sugar', 'salt' or 'vegetable oil', for example, it's not going to be a healthy product. If we are buying a pasta sauce, we will look for one that contains 'tomatoes and salt', or even better, just 'tomatoes'. We also avoid artificial sweeteners (these usually appear as the term 'sweetener' followed by a number).

After looking at the ingredients, we look at the nutritional panel. Make sure you check how many recommended serves there are per pack. Sometimes if you look at the sugar per serve, and that is 5 g, you might think this sounds low. However, if the bottle contains four serves, the sugar content of the entire product is 4 x 5 g = 20 g.

Avoid foods with trans-fats in the nutritional panel — these are highly-processed fats with no nutritional benefits. Try to stick to products that are low in sugar and, if possible, stick to products sweetened with natural sugars such as those that come from dates, coconut sugar, rice malt syrup, etc.

HEALTHY SUBSTITUTIONS

Healthy substitutions are your best friends when it comes to preparing healthy meals and snacks. We don't believe in depriving ourselves, so if we are craving something like lasagne, or a schnitzel or chocolate chip cookies — we'll have them! But we try to switch a few ingredients to make the meal healthier than the traditional version (though just as tasty).

OUR FAVOURITE HEALTHY FOOD SWAPS

PASTA

zucchini noodles (shaved zucchini)
or mixed pasta and zucchini

FLOUR

almond meal or a mix of almond meal
and flour for nutritional benefits

BUTTER AND OIL IN BAKING

a combination of natural yoghurt/
butter/oil

MAYO

natural yoghurt

PROCESSED SALAD DRESSINGS

whisked lemon juice or balsamic
vinegar and olive oil

REFINED SUGAR

dates/bananas; a small amount of rice
malt syrup or maple syrup in baking

BREADCRUMBS

almond meal for coating schnitzels

LASAGNE SHEETS

eggplant or mixed pasta and eggplant

SWEETENED FAT-FREE YOGHURT

full-fat unsweetened natural yoghurt

MILK CHOCOLATE

70 per cent cocoa dark chocolate

CHEESE ON PASTA OR IN SAUCES

nutritional yeast or a combination
of nutritional yeast/cheese

SOFT DRINK

mineral water with your favourite
fruit

FRUIT JUICE

a homemade smoothie (page 178);
the fibre from the fruit will keep
you full

ICE CREAM

homemade ice cream (page 214)

WHAT IS IN OUR FRIDGE?

Our keep-cool essentials

SPINACH
(fresh and frozen, perfect
in smoothies and salads)

AVOCADO
(an amazing source of healthy fat)

TOMATOES

ZUCCHINI

EGGPLANT

STEPH one of my favourite ways to
make a salad more interesting is
to chop up some eggplant, haloumi
and capsicum, grill them on a barbie
or in a pan with some olive oil and
chuck them on top. Yum!

HALOUMI OR FETA
(who doesn't love cheese?
In moderation, of course)

NATURAL/GREEK YOGHURT

UNSWEETENED ALMOND MILK

KIMCHI + SAUERKRAUT
(hello healthy gut!)

KOMBUCHA

FREE-RANGE EGGS

BERRIES
(perfect for smoothies or as a quick
snack with yoghurt)

WHAT IS IN OUR PANTRY?
Go-to ingredients

EXTRA VIRGIN OLIVE OIL

HIMALAYAN PINK SALT

TINNED TUNA IN OLIVE OIL
(perfect as a quick protein-packed snack and great on top of a salad for an easy healthy meal)

PEPITAS
(we love roasting these and adding to salads for some crunch)

MACA POWDER
(we add this to our smoothies – it is said to be great for balancing hormones naturally)

SPIRULINA POWDER

CHIA SEEDS
(these are great added to smoothies or in a delicious chia pudding)

POPCORN KERNELS
(we make our own popcorn when we feel like a healthy treat or snack)

NUT BUTTER
(used in a lot of healthy baking recipes)
STEPH I literally have peanut butter every day, in smoothies, on toast or with fruit. My 'go-to' afternoon snack is sliced apple with peanut butter on top!

BANANAS
(perfect for smoothies, in baking, and on their own as an amazing pick-me-up)

APPLES
(handy to grab and eat on the go)

10.
Recipes

Breakfast

Acai bowl

Serves 1

There's a good reason Acai became so popular! Not only does it make you feel like you're eating sorbet for brekkie, but it's super nutritious too. Acai (much like all other berries) improves blood circulation in the body, fills you with energy, is packed with antioxidants and is a great source of dietary fibre. Play around with different toppings until you find the perfect way to start your day!

⅔ cup (100 g) frozen Acai
1 frozen banana
A dash of almond milk

1 Place all the ingredients in a food processor and blend until smooth.
2 Serve immediately with your favourite toppings.

Laura's favourite topping: Greek yoghurt, berries and coconut flakes for extra crunch

Steph's favourite topping: chopped almonds, a sprinkle of goji berries, 1 tsp cacao nibs and 1 tsp chia seeds

Supergreen
brekkie salad

Serves 1

Do you love eggs for brekkie but are
tired of the ol' eggs on toast with
sides? Or maybe you're a salad fan
and feel like a salad most mornings?
Our brekkie salad is super-filling
and incredibly nutritious. Don't let
the kale scare you away! We LOVE this
recipe. The dressing on the kale,
combined with the oozy yolk from the
egg, the creamy goat's cheese and the
crunch of the pepitas is a match made
in heaven.

1 large handful roughly torn
  kale leaves

1 tsp olive oil

Juice of ½ lemon

2 eggs

¼ cup (50 g) quinoa, cooked

¼ avocado, chopped

1 tsp finely chopped chilli

1 Tbsp goat's cheese

1 Tbsp roasted pepitas (pumpkin
  seeds)

1   Place the kale in a medium-sized
    bowl with the olive oil and lemon
    juice. Massage the oil and juice
    into the kale for 60-90 seconds
    or until the kale has turned
    darker and the oil and lemon juice
    have been absorbed.

2   Poach or fry the eggs however you
    like them.

3   Add the quinoa, avocado, chilli,
    goat's cheese and pepitas to the
    bowl of kale and top with the
    cooked eggs. Season with salt
    and pepper to taste.

Chilli scrambled eggs

Serves 1

Some mornings we just crave eggs and this combo is one of our faves. It is inspired by the cafes of Melbourne, as this is always a menu staple and makes for the perfect weekend breakfast. The homemade version is even more special. If you're a chilli lover, try this next time you whip up some eggs: we promise you will be blissfully surprised.

2 whole eggs, lightly beaten

1 egg white, lightly beaten

Dash of milk (optional)

¼ fresh red chilli, finely chopped

1 tsp butter

1 Tbsp chilli-infused extra virgin olive oil

1   Whisk the eggs with the milk and a pinch of sea salt.

2   Add the chilli.

3   Heat the butter in a small frying pan and, once melted, pour in the egg mixture.

4   Gently fold the eggs together as they cook. After 30-60 seconds, when there is no liquid egg visible, remove from the pan.

5   Drizzle chilli oil over the eggs and serve.

Chocolate granola

Makes approx. 500 g of granola. We recommend 3 Tbsp of this as a meal with your favourite yoghurt/fruit combo or 1 Tbsp sprinkled on your smoothie/acai bowl.

This is the perfect Sunday baking recipe to set you up for the week. Put it in a jar and you can have delicious and healthy granola every day. It's important to know that most store-bought granola is packed with sugar and is almost no better for you than those sweet cereals from your childhood. So with this in mind, we make our own. It is much cheaper and the best part is you can mix and match nuts or seeds to make it perfectly matched to you!

2 Tbsp coconut oil

2 Tbsp rice malt syrup

1 Tbsp cacao powder

1 tsp vanilla extract

1 cup (195 g) buckwheat

½ cup (65 g) slivered almonds

½ cup (80 g) roughly chopped raw almonds

½ cup (30 g) coconut flakes

3 Tbsp sesame seeds

3 Tbsp chia seeds

1 Preheat the oven to 200°C (400°F) and line a large baking tray or dish with baking paper.

2 In a small saucepan over medium heat, melt together the coconut oil, rice malt syrup, cacao powder and vanilla.

3 Pour in the rest of the ingredients and mix well.

4 Spread the granola mix evenly across the tray and bake for 30–40 minutes, stirring every 10 minutes, or until golden brown.

5 Cool completely and store in a sealed container for up to 2 weeks.

6 Serve with natural Greek yoghurt and berries or bananas.

OMELETTE THREE WAYS

Each omelette serves 1

Omelettes are great because they're easy to chuck together quickly from whatever's in your fridge! They're also not just for breakfast... if we haven't got anything prepared for dinner we'll usually have some eggs and veggies, so these omelettes can be quick, nutritious dinners as well.

Note: Eggs are one of nature's star snack foods. Full of good protein and healthy fats

Chive and goat's cheese with smoked salmon

2 eggs, lightly beaten
1 Tbsp finely chopped chives
Chilli flakes, to taste
1 tsp olive oil or butter
1 Tbsp goat's cheese, crumbled
2-3 slices smoked salmon

1   Whisk together the eggs then mix in the chives. Add the chilli flakes, sea salt and pepper.

2   Heat the oil or butter in a small frying pan for 30-60 seconds until warm. Pour in the egg mixture to spread over the base of the pan. When the top of the omelette has no runny egg left, sprinkle with goat's cheese and fold one half over the other in the pan.

3   Transfer to a plate and serve with the smoked salmon.

Spinach and herb

½ zucchini (courgette)
2 eggs, lightly beaten
1 handful basil leaves
1 handful chopped spinach leaves
Chilli flakes, to taste
1 tsp olive oil or butter
1 Tbsp goat's cheese, crumbled
½ avocado, sliced

1 Grate the zucchini and leave in a colander to drain. Squeeze out the moisture with your hands, then pat dry in paper towel. (This prevents water running into the omelette from the zucchini.)

2 In a food processor or with a stick mixer, blend the eggs and basil until smooth. Transfer to a bowl.

3 Add the spinach to the bowl, then the chilli flakes, and season with sea salt and pepper to taste. Mix in the zucchini.

4 Heat the oil or butter in a small frying pan for 30-60 seconds until warm. Pour in the egg mixture to spread over the base of the pan. When the top of the omelette has no runny egg left, sprinkle with goat's cheese and fold in half.

5 Transfer to a plate and serve with avocado.

Ham and cheese

2 eggs, lightly beaten
1-2 slices of ham, chopped
1 tsp butter
1 Tbsp shaved parmesan cheese

1 Whisk the eggs together, then add the ham.

2 Heat the butter in a small frying pan for 30-60 seconds until warm. Pour in the egg mixture to spread over the base of the pan. When the top of the omelette has no runny egg left, sprinkle with parmesan and fold one half over the other.

3 Season with salt and pepper, transfer to a plate and serve.

PANCAKES THREE WAYS

Because: PANCAKES! Who doesn't get those random pancake cravings? That kind of urge is hard to handle, so next time, instead of trying to ignore it (or giving in to a packet mix filled with nasties) make these. They're quick, easy and super-tasty. These are the perfect special weekend breakfast to serve with loved ones, or, of course, to treat yourself.

Sweet potato

Serves 2

½ cup (75 g) peeled and diced sweet potato

¼ cup (25 g) almond meal

2 eggs, lightly beaten

¼ tsp cinnamon

¼ cup (60 ml) almond milk

1 tsp baking powder

1 medjool date, pitted, or 2 tsp maple syrup

1 tsp coconut oil or butter, for cooking

1 Steam the sweet potato, drain and refrigerate to cool for 15-20 minutes.

2 Transfer into a blender or food processor along with the almond meal, eggs, cinnamon, almond milk, baking powder and date or maple syrup and blend until smooth.

3 Heat the coconut oil or butter in a frying pan over medium heat. Once hot, pour in the pancake mix to your desired pancake size. (We recommend about 2 tablespoons per pancake to make them easy to flip.)

4 Cook for around 1 minute, or until bubbles form on the surface, then flip over.

5 Cook for another 30 seconds, until both sides are slightly golden.

6 Remove from the pan and serve hot!

Protein packed

Serves 1

- 2 eggs, lightly beaten
- 1 heaped Tbsp Greek yoghurt
- 1 Tbsp coconut flour
- 1 tsp baking powder
- 1 scoop (30 g) vanilla protein powder
- 1 tsp rice malt syrup or Natvia
- 1 tsp coconut oil or butter

1 Combine the eggs, yoghurt, coconut flour, baking powder, protein powder and rice malt syrup or Natvia in a mixing bowl.

2 Heat the coconut oil or butter in a frying pan over medium heat. Once hot, pour in the pancake mix to your desired pancake size. (We recommend about 1-2 table-spoons per pancake to make them easy to flip.)

3 Cook for around 1 minute, or until bubbles form on the surface, then flip over.

4 Cook for another 30 seconds, until both sides are slightly golden.

5 Remove from the pan and serve hot!

Two-ingredient pancakes

Serves 1

- 2 eggs, lightly beaten
- 1 ripe banana, mashed
- 1 tsp coconut oil or butter

1 In a mixing bowl, whisk together the eggs and banana until they reach a smooth consistency.

2 Heat the coconut oil or butter in a frying pan over medium heat. Once hot, pour in the pancake mix to your desired pancake size. (We recommend about 1 tablespoon per pancake to make them easy to flip.)

3 Cook for around 1 minute, or until bubbles form on the surface, then flip over.

4 Cook for another 30 seconds, until both sides are slightly golden.

5 Remove from the pan and serve hot!

note: If your protein powder is naturally sweetened, you will not need to add any sweetening syrup to this

Brekkie cups

Makes 6

Are you a savoury breakfast person? Not into sweet things in the morning, but need something quick and easy on the go? Then our brekkie cups are the perfect treat for you. We love this recipe because you can prepare it the night before, or make a batch on a Sunday evening to last through the first half of the week. This recipe not only makes mornings easier, but is also super-easy with minimal prep needed.

Extra virgin olive oil, for
  brushing
6 bacon rashers
6 eggs
1 handful basil leaves, sliced
1 handful cherry tomatoes, halved
3 Tbsp goat's cheese

1 Preheat the oven to 180°C (350°F) fan-forced.

2 Prepare a 6-cup medium-sized muffin tray by brushing all sides with olive oil or lining with baking paper.

3 Line each cup with a bacon rasher.

4 Crack one egg into the centre of each bacon-lined cup.

5 Add an even amount of basil and tomatoes to each cup and then sprinkle goat's cheese evenly over the top.

6 Place the tray in the oven and cook for 15–20 minutes (or until egg is cooked through and bacon crisp). Keep in an airtight container in the fridge for up to 3 days.

Banana and choc-chia pudding

Serves 1

Chia pudding is the perfect choice if you are time-poor in the morning. Maybe you don't have time to make anything for breakfast, or you go straight from the gym or training to your office/school in the morning? This is so easy to make! It's best made the night before too, so that way you can just grab and go in the morning. Chia seeds are a great source of Omega 3 and healthy fats to keep you going all morning.

1 cup (250 ml) coconut or almond milk

3 Tbsp chia seeds

1 tsp raw cacao powder

¼ tsp vanilla extract

1 banana, chopped

1 Combine the milk, chia seeds, cacao powder and vanilla in a small bowl or jar.

2 Stir in the chopped banana and put in the fridge. Leave to set for a minimum of 2-3 hours or overnight.

Note: If you're having this post workout, add a scoop (30 g) of protein powder to the mix

Perfect porridge

Serves 1

This porridge is really simple and incredibly satisfying. Buckwheat is a gluten-free grain that is packed with fibre, practically fat-free and provides a high source of amino acids, protein, antioxidants, vitamins and minerals. Fill up your belly with the good stuff and start your day off right. These are our favourite toppings, but feel free to add whatever fruit or nuts you prefer. To make this vegan-friendly, you can use almond or oat milk instead of cow's milk, rice malt syrup instead of honey, and swap the yoghurt out for a dairy-free option too.

We love this recipe because it's like a hug in a bowl. It makes cold winter mornings something we look forward to. There's nothing better than curling up with a blanket and a bowl of our perfect porridge when it's freezing outside.

¼ cup (40 g) buckwheat flakes
¼ tsp ground cinnamon
¼ cup (60 ml) milk of choice
1 Tbsp honey
1 Tbsp peanut butter (or almond)
1 cup (155 g) blueberries, fresh or frozen
1 Tbsp Greek yoghurt

1   Put the buckwheat flakes, cinnamon, and ¾ cup (190 ml) water into a small saucepan.

2   Bring to the boil, then reduce to a simmer, cover, and cook for around 5-8 minutes, stirring occasionally, until all the water has been absorbed.

3   Remove from the heat and stir in the milk and honey.

4   Transfer to a bowl and top with the peanut butter, blueberries and yoghurt.

Note: Buckwheat helps boost your energy levels and lower cholesterol

Smoothies + Snacks

SMOOTHIES

All of our smoothies serve 1

Smoothies are great if you're busy but craving a filling and nutritious snack to go. Keep your favourite ingredients handy in your fridge and pantry, so they're ready when you are! We have smoothies every day in summer. They're also a perfect 3pm pick-me-up when you feel like something sweet.

Choc'aholic

1 tsp cacao powder

1 banana (frozen works best)

½ cup (125 ml) unsweetened almond milk

1 Tbsp protein powder (optional)

1 handful ice cubes

1 Mix all ingredients in a blender until smooth. Serve immediately.

B1 & B2 (berries & banana)

½ cup (80 g) blueberries (frozen works best)

½ banana (frozen works best)

½ cup (125 ml) unsweetened almond milk

1 heaped Tbsp Greek yoghurt

1 Place all ingredients in the blender until smooth and then serve immediately.

Salted caramel

1 medjool date, pitted

1 tsp nut butter

½ banana (frozen works best)

½ cup (125 ml) unsweetened almond milk

1 Place all ingredients in the blender until smooth and then serve immediately.

Nutty Popeye

1 handful baby spinach leaves

1 Tbsp peanut butter

½ banana (frozen works best)

¾ cup (185 ml) unsweetened almond milk

1 Tbsp maca powder

1 medjool date, pitted

1 Place all ingredients in the blender until smooth and then serve immediately.

Sweet and sour muffins

Makes 12

We LOVE making our own muffins. Unfortunately, store-bought and café-made muffins are likely to be packed with refined sugar that can give you a quick high followed by an energy lull. So, if you're a morning muffin person, it's best to make them yourself – they are so easy, there is no excuse. Not only are these a delicious snack, they're also a great source of healthy fats which will keep you feeling full for longer. They're a perfect afternoon treat to have with a big mug of tea and keep you going until dinnertime. These flavours are a favourite with both our families: we all love the perfect combination of lemony citrus tartness and blueberry sweetness, but you can use different berries.

2 eggs, lightly beaten

2 Tbsp lemon juice

1 Tbsp grated lemon zest

½ cup (125 ml) almond milk

½ cup (125 g) natural Greek yoghurt

2 Tbsp rice malt syrup

1 cup (125 g) gluten-free flour

¾ cup (80 g) almond meal

1 tsp baking powder

1 cup (155 g) blueberries

1 Preheat the oven to 180°C (350°F) and line a medium-sized muffin tray with 12 patty pans or baking paper.

2 In a mixing bowl, whisk together the eggs, lemon juice and zest, almond milk, yoghurt and rice malt syrup.

3 Add the flour, almond meal and baking powder to the mixture and stir with a wooden spoon until combined. Gently fold through the blueberries.

4 Evenly distribute the mixture between the patty pans and transfer tray to the oven. Bake for 20-24 minutes or until the muffins are golden brown and cooked through. Store in an airtight container for up to 3 days.

Vanilla and coconut bliss balls

Makes 12-15 bliss balls

Bliss balls are so handy to have ready to go in your fridge. Whether you're running out the door in the morning and don't have time for breakfast, or you need an afternoon pick-me-up, or even a pre- or post-workout snack.

These bliss balls are very close to our hearts, as they are one of the first recipes we created when we started our cooking journey. While we have come a long way since then, bliss balls are the one thing we felt we could always get right! No baking required, just blending. If you find your bliss balls are too dry, simply add a little water and, if they are too wet, add a little extra shredded coconut and almond meal.

1 cup (65 g) shredded coconut
1 tsp vanilla extract
½ cup (60 g) vanilla protein powder
½ cup (80 g) pitted and chopped medjool dates
½ cup (50 g) almond meal
1 Tbsp coconut oil

1 Put all the ingredients in a food processor and mix on low speed. If the mixture is too dry to come together, add a dash of water.

2 Once the ingredients are completely combined and have formed a large ball in the food processor, switch off.

3 Roll the mixture into small balls with your hands (wet your hands with warm water before you start, to prevent the mixture sticking). Store in the fridge for up to 4 days.

Note: Almond meal is a fantastic subsitute for regular flour. Almonds provide more calcium than any other nut

DIP N STICKS

Each recipe serves 4

Want to put out snacks you know your guests will enjoy, but also want to make sure they're still nutritious so everyone can walk away smiling? These are a few of our favourite healthy dips to have ready for your guests. They can always be paired with some brown rice crackers too. We love these when we get home from a long day at work - we eat them with some chopped carrot, celery or capsicum, or most importantly as part of one of our beloved cheese platters.

Spinach and feta

1 single serve packet (150 g) frozen spinach, thawed and finely chopped

Juice of ½ lemon

2 Tbsp olive oil

1 cup (250 g) Greek yoghurt

½ cup (65 g) crumbled feta cheese

1 Mix together all the ingredients until the dip has a smooth consistency. Add sea salt to taste.

2 Serve with veggie sticks or your favourite healthy crackers.

Beetroot hummus

1 large beetroot

400 g (14 oz) tin chickpeas, rinsed and drained

1½ Tbsp tahini

Juice of ½ lemon

1 tsp cumin

1 Tbsp olive oil

1 Peel, chop then steam the beetroot for 30-40 minutes, until tender.

2 Blend the beetroot with all the other ingredients in a food processor until smooth. Add sea salt to taste.

3 Serve with veggie sticks or your favourite healthy crackers.

HEALTHY ICY POLES 3 WAYS

Each recipe makes 6 icy poles

Our creamy icy poles are the perfect summer treat. They're easy to make and a wonderful healthy option when you want something sweet and delicious to cool you down.

Green

1 cup (50 g) baby spinach leaves
2 bananas
1 cup (250 ml) coconut milk

1 Blend all the ingredients in a food processor until smooth.
2 Pour into icy pole trays and place in the freezer for 2-3 hours, or until set.

Choc banana

1 Tbsp cacao powder
2 bananas
1 cup (250 ml) coconut milk

1 Blend all the ingredients in a food processor until smooth.
2 Pour into icy pole trays and place in the freezer for 2-3 hours, or until set.

Strawberry coconut

1 cup (150 g) strawberries
1 banana
1 cup (250 ml) coconut milk

1 Blend all the ingredients in a food processor until smooth.
2 Pour into icy pole trays and place in the freezer for 2-3 hours, or until set.

Crunchy chicken schnitzel

Serves 4

This is one of our favourite recipes. Chicken schnitzel was a staple in both our households when we were growing up. Our healthy version is just as delicious as the classic (but means we no longer have to go to the local pub to satisfy those schnitty cravings). Plus, these have been thoroughly boyfriend-approved!

2 chicken breasts (500 g)
½ cup (50 g) almond meal
1 handful finely chopped parsley
1 egg, lightly beaten
Olive oil for frying
1 handful sliced leg ham
3 tomatoes, thinly sliced
Feta or goat's cheese

1 Preheat the oven to 180°C (350°F) and line a baking tray with baking paper.

2 Slice the chicken breasts lengthways into 3-4 small thin pieces per breast.

3 In a shallow bowl, mix together the almond meal and parsley with a pinch of sea salt.

4 Pour the beaten egg into a separate shallow bowl.

5 Dip each chicken piece into the egg to cover. Shake off the excess egg. Then press each chicken piece into the ground almond mix to form a coating.

6 Heat a dash of olive oil in a frying pan over medium heat. Brown each piece of chicken for 1-2 minutes on each side. Transfer to the lined baking tray.

7 Top each piece of chicken with a slice of ham, top with a slice or two of tomato and then sprinkle with your choice of cheese. Bake in the oven for 10-15 minutes or until the cheese has started to brown and the chicken is cooked through.

8 Serve with a big green salad, cauliflower rice, sweet potato chippies or any of your favourite healthy fries.

One-pan baked chicken

Serves 4

Who else hates doing the dishes?
Less washing up is always better,
we think, and this one-pan recipe
is a super-simple, quick dish that
everyone will enjoy. Chicken is a
great protein source that is low in
fat and full of great vitamins and
minerals. This meal is also packed
with flavour from the beautiful
cherry tomatoes and Kalamata olives.
We love serving this with a big side
salad or some cauliflower rice.

1 Tbsp olive oil

Juice of ½ lemon

2 chicken breasts (500 g)

1 punnet (250 g) cherry tomatoes,
halved

¼ cup (40 g) pitted kalamata
olives

1   Preheat the oven to 200°C (400°F)
    and line a tray with baking paper.

2   Combine the olive oil, lemon
    juice, and sea salt and pepper to
    taste in a small bowl.

3   Rub the chicken breasts with the
    oil and juice, then arrange them
    evenly in the tray.

4   Spread the cherry tomatoes and
    olives around the chicken breasts.

5   Bake for 25–30 minutes or until
    the chicken is golden brown and
    cooked through.

Flavoursome baked fish

Serves 4

Fish is one of our most-loved protein sources, and this is our favourite way to prepare it. This recipe is SUPER-easy, so we have it at least once a week! We like to use salmon, but your favourite kind of fish will work just as well. You can wrap each portion in baking paper, or you can put them all on one baking tray. We love to pair this with cauliflower rice and some kimchi or a big leafy salad. Once you have the fish in the oven, you can prepare your sides.

4 salmon fillets (or fish of your choice)

1 bunch flat-leaf parsley, finely chopped

½ red onion, finely chopped

1 small red chilli, finely chopped

Juice of 1 lemon

3 Tbsp minced garlic

1 punnet (250 g) cherry tomatoes, halved

1 Preheat the oven to 180°C (350°F) and line a baking tray with baking paper.

2 Put the fish fillets into the baking tray.

3 Mix together the parsley, onion and chilli with the lemon juice, garlic, and sea salt and pepper to taste. Arrange evenly over and between the fillets.

4 Scatter the cherry tomatoes evenly around the tray.

5 Bake for 20–25 minutes (depending on how well done you like your fish).

6 Serve with your sides of choice.

Steph's spicy stir-fry

Serves 4

Stir-fries are one of our absolute favourites because they're so simple and so delicious! This is Steph's go-to version, but you can totally whip one up with any vegetables and protein that you wish. It's a great one to fall back on if you have to work with leftovers in your fridge.

½ cup (35 g) shredded coconut

1 tsp sesame seeds

½ cup (80 g) cashew nuts

2 Tbsp coconut oil

2 x 400 g chicken breasts, cut into bite-size pieces

½ head purple cabbage, shredded

1 carrot, chopped

1 zucchini (courgette), chopped

1 capsicum (red pepper), chopped

1 chilli, finely chopped (seeds optional for extra spice)

2 Tbsp tamari

1 tsp paprika

½ Tbsp turmeric

1 Warm a frying pan over medium heat. Toast the shredded coconut, sesame seeds and cashews until golden. Tip out and set aside.

2 Heat half the coconut oil in the pan. Add the chicken and fry, stirring regularly so it cooks evenly, until cooked through.

3 Stir in the cabbage, carrot, zucchini, capsicum and chilli.

4 Add the rest of the coconut oil, along with the tamari, paprika and turmeric and stir for 2–3 minutes, or until the veggies are cooked.

5 Remove from the heat and sprinkle the toasted coconut, nuts and sesame seeds on top.

Pesto zoodles

Serves 2 as main or 4 as a side

I mean who doesn't love pesto? When
you have the awesome flavour of pesto
chicken, zoodles taste just like
pasta! Swapping the pasta out for
zucchini is a great way to lighten
any of your favourite recipes. You
can have this as a side with grilled
chicken or salmon, or you can add
shredded chicken into the saucepan
at Step 3 to have it as a main meal.
This one will have you licking the
bowl clean!

2 zucchini (courgettes),
  spiralised or grated

¼ cup (40 g) whole almonds

1 bunch basil leaves

Juice of 1 lemon

3 Tbsp olive oil

1 punnet (250 g) cherry tomatoes,
  halved

10 black olives

1   Strain the zucchini in a colander,
    then squeeze out the excess
    moisture with your hands. Pat the
    zucchini dry with paper towel.

2   To make the pesto, blend the
    almonds, basil, lemon juice,
    olive oil and sea salt to taste
    until smooth in a food processor
    or blender.

3   Heat a frying pan over medium
    heat and add the pesto, cherry
    tomatoes and olives. Stir-fry
    for 3-4 minutes and then add the
    zucchini. Stir for 30-60 seconds,
    serve and enjoy!

Sprout salad

Serves 4 as a side

Did you try Brussels sprouts when you were a kid and turn up your nose at them? If you haven't tried them since, give them another go. You'll be pleasantly surprised with how delicious they can be when they're cooked right. We love serving this with salmon or chicken.

500 g (1 lb) Brussels sprouts, washed and chopped into quarters

2 handfuls spinach leaves, roughly chopped

1 avocado, diced

1 red chilli, finely chopped

1 Tbsp olive oil

1 tsp tahini

1 Tbsp apple cider vinegar

Juice of ½ lemon

1 tsp olive oil, for frying

2 Tbsp pepitas (pumpkin seeds)

1 Preheat the oven to 220°C (425°F) and line a tray with baking paper.

2 Arrange the sprouts on the tray, season with sea salt to taste and bake for 20–25 minutes or until golden and crunchy.

3 While the sprouts are baking, toss together the spinach, avocado and chilli in a salad bowl.

4 In a small jar or bowl, combine the olive oil, tahini, apple cider vinegar and lemon juice. Add sea salt and pepper to taste and whisk until combined.

5 Heat the olive oil in a frying pan on high heat and toast the pepitas until golden brown.

6 Once the sprouts have finished baking, for 5 minutes then add to the salad. Add the dressing, toss to combine, and sprinkle the pepitas on top.

Easy eggplant parmigiana

Serves 5-6

Tastes the same as the classic — okay maybe not quite as cheesy, but we're looking after you! We absolutely LOVE roasted eggplant. And it's quite unbeatable when it's layered with these flavours. Laura lived in Italy for a time and this was her favourite dinner dish. The delicious hot eggplant, combined with a beautiful homemade tomato sauce is a match made in heaven. We love pairing this with a big leafy salad.

3 Tbsp olive oil

3 large eggplants (aubergines), sliced horizontally into thin circles

1 brown onion, diced

2 garlic cloves, minced

2 x 400 g (14 oz) tins diced tomatoes

1-2 tsp chilli flakes (or to taste)

1½ cups (345 g) ricotta cheese

6-8 basil leaves

1 Line an ovenproof dish with baking paper and preheat the oven to 180°C (350°F).

2 Heat 2 tablespoons of the olive oil in a large pan (or on a barbecue or grill plate) and grill both sides of the eggplant in batches for 1-2 minutes on each side, until the flesh turns golden. Remove from the pan.

3 In the same pan, add the onion, along with the rest of the olive oil and the garlic. Fry, stirring, until the onion has browned. Add the tomatoes, chilli, and a pinch of sea salt, then turn the heat to low and simmer for 20-25 minutes.

4 Arrange a layer of eggplant slices in the base of the dish. Pour on a layer of sauce, add a further layer of eggplant, then more sauce, building up the layers until you've used all the eggplant and all the sauce.

5 Smooth the ricotta evenly on top and bake for 50-60 minutes.

6 Once cooked, scatter the basil leaves over the top and serve.

Grilled veggie salad with haloumi

Serves 2

Do you make friends with salad? We understand not everyone's a big salad fan, but this one is pretty finger lick'n good! We've kept it vego-friendly, but if you like you could totally add some chicken on top.

½ eggplant (aubergine), cut into bite-sized chunks

1 capsicum (red pepper), sliced into strips

40 g (1½ oz) haloumi, cut into bite-sized chunks

1 Tbsp tamari

2 Tbsp olive oil

2 big handfuls baby spinach leaves

Juice of ½ lemon

1 Put the eggplant, capsicum and haloumi into a bowl. Add the tamari, along with a pinch of salt and pepper and half of the olive oil. Mix to evenly coat the vegetables and haloumi.

2 Heat a large grill pan (or the barbecue). Once hot, grill the eggplant, capsicum and haloumi until golden.

3 Transfer to a salad bowl, stir in the spinach, then drizzle with the rest of the olive oil and the lemon juice. Too easy!

Coconut fried rice

Serves 2

Next time you're about to call your local Chinese restaurant for some take-away, check your fridge for these items. I bet you will have all of them — or at least most. So how about you chuck your own fried rice together instead?

1 cup (250 ml) coconut milk
1 cup (200 g) brown rice
1 cup (140 g) frozen peas
3 Tbsp coconut oil
1 chicken breast, chopped into small pieces
2 carrots, diced
5 spring onions, finely chopped
½ cup (35 g) shredded coconut
2 Tbsp tamari
1 handful spinach, roughly chopped

1   Pour the coconut milk and 1 cup (250 ml) water into a saucepan over high heat. Bring to the boil.

2   Add the rice and reduce heat to medium-low so that the rice is simmering. Cover the pan. Once the rice has absorbed all the liquid, set aside to cool.

3   While the rice is cooking, cook the peas in boiling water, following the packet instructions. Drain and set aside.

4   Heat 1 tablespoon of the coconut oil in a large frying pan. Fry the chicken for 2-3 minutes or until golden and cooked through. Remove from the pan and set aside.

5   Add the rest of the coconut oil to the pan along with the carrot, spring onion, shredded coconut and cooked peas. Toss for 2 minutes, then add the rice, tamari and chicken and toss for 1 minute.

6   Finally, toss through spinach for 30 seconds and serve.

Slow-cooked lamb

Serves 6

There's nothing like a juicy delicious slow-cooked lamb, right? Let this melt in your mouth and thank us later. We personally love slow-cooked lamb served with a side of sweet potato mash and steamed broccolini.

2 Tbsp olive oil

1 kg (2 lb 4 oz) lamb shoulder

1 Tbsp minced garlic

Juice of 1 lemon

1 Tbsp dried oregano

1   Preheat the oven to 160°C (320°F) and line a large roasting tin (big enough to fit the lamb) with baking paper.

2   Heat half of the olive oil in a large frying pan. Fry the lamb for 1-2 minutes on each side to brown.

3   Transfer the lamb to the baking tray. Rub the lamb with garlic, lemon juice, the remaining olive oil, and sea salt and pepper to taste. Sprinkle with the oregano. Cover the tray with foil.

4   Roast in the oven for 3-4 hours or until the lamb is cooked through and falling off the bone.

Legendary lamb salad

Serves 2

This truly is LEGENDARY, we promise. We guarantee whoever you whip this up for will be wanting more. Lamb is filled with healthy fats, is a strong source of iron, and of course it's packed with protein! So ditch the urge to grab a kebab and make this instead.

1 tsp olive oil

350 g (12 oz) lamb backstrap

2 tsp pine nuts

400 g (14 oz) tin cannellini beans, rinsed and drained

½ punnet (120 g) cherry tomatoes, cut in quarters

1 Lebanese cucumber, peeled and diced

30 g (1 oz) black olives, chopped

80 g (3 oz) baby spinach leaves

2 Tbsp tzatziki

1 Preheat the oven to 160°C (320°F).

2 Rub oil over the lamb with your hands and season with salt and pepper to taste.

3 Heat a frying pan over medium-high heat and sear the lamb all over (approximately 1–2 minutes on each side).

4 Transfer to an ovenproof dish and roast in the oven for 5–8 minutes. Remove from the oven and cover the lamb loosely with foil. Set it aside on your benchtop to rest.

5 Toast the pine nuts in a hot dry pan for 1–2 minutes until they are golden.

6 While the lamb rests, toss the beans, tomato, cucumber, olives and spinach with the tzatziki, season with salt and pepper and divide between two plates.

7 Cut the lamb into slices, arrange on top of the salads and top with pine nuts.

Clean choc-chip cookies

Makes 12-15 cookies

This is the recipe that started it all! This was one of the first recipes we worked on together and it is still one of our most regularly made, too. We just can't get enough of these, and we're sure all you other cookie monsters and your friends and family out there will love them too! If you would like to make these vegan-friendly, swap the Greek yoghurt for 1 extra tablespoon of coconut oil. For paleo peeps out there, you can also swap the choc chip pieces for cacao nibs.

1 cup (120 g) spelt flour (or gluten-free flour)

⅔ cup (70 g) almond meal

6 medjool dates, pitted

⅓ cup (100 g) Greek yoghurt

2 Tbsp almond butter

2 Tbsp rice malt syrup

1 tsp vanilla extract

6 Tbsp coconut oil

1 tsp baking powder

½ cup (50 g) finely chopped dark chocolate (85 per cent cocoa)

1   Preheat the oven to 180°C (350°F) and line a baking tray with baking paper.

2   In a food processor, mix the flour, almond meal and dates on high speed to form a paste.

3   Add the yoghurt, almond butter, rice malt syrup, vanilla, coconut oil and baking powder and blend again on high to combine. The mixture should be quite doughy. Fold in the chocolate with a wooden spoon.

4   On a clean work surface, roll tablespoons of mixture into small balls and transfer them to the tray. Use the back of a wet tablespoon to flatten the balls into cookies.

5   Bake for 12-13 minutes, but start checking from about 11 minutes – they burn very quickly!

6   Once cooked, removed from the oven and leave to cool as long as you can resist.

Homestyle apple crumble

Serves 8

This recipe reminds us of the wonderful aroma of baked apple pies from the local bakery when we were kids. We wanted to create a recipe as a tribute to those memories, but also something nourishing with no refined sugar. We simply love cooking with fruit because it makes baking naturally sweet without the need to add large amounts of other sweeteners. It's the perfect sweet treat in the colder months, particularly for a dinner party. If you have any guests with a super-sweet tooth, they can add a scoop of ice-cream. We personally love a scoop of natural yoghurt with ours.

8 apples, cored and sliced into thin wedges

1 tsp cinnamon

2 Tbsp rice malt syrup

¾ cup (120 g) natural almonds

½ cup (60 g) walnuts

4 medjool dates, pitted

½ cup (30 g) coconut flakes

2 Tbsp coconut oil

1 cup (155 g) blueberries

1   Preheat the oven to 180°C (350°F).

2   Put the apples in a saucepan over medium heat with the cinnamon and 2 teaspoons of the rice malt syrup, along with a ½ cup (125 ml) of water. Bring to the boil and then turn down to low and simmer for 10-15 minutes or until the apples are soft and almost all of the water has been absorbed.

3   Combine the almonds, walnuts, dates, coconut, coconut oil and remaining syrup in a food processor. Blitz for 30 seconds or until the nuts have roughly broken down.

4   Place cooked apple into a baking dish and stir through the blueberries.

5   Cover the apples with the crumble mix and bake in the oven for 20-25 minutes, or until crumble is golden brown. Serve hot!

Moreish choc popcorn

Serves 4 (or 1-2 if you're a popcorn lover like Steph)

Steph's a creature of habit, and chocolate covered popcorn is certainly one of her most regular treats! There's nothing quite like a sweet and salty combo. Just have a napkin handy – this gets a little messy.

30 g dark chocolate (85 per cent)
3 Tbsp coconut oil
1 cup (220 g) popcorn kernels
Pink salt (to taste)

1 Melt the chocolate in a small saucepan over low heat. It can burn easily, so stir constantly and remove from the heat as soon as it has melted through.

2 Pour the coconut oil into a large saucepan over medium heat. Drop a few corn kernels in the oil to test the heat – if small bubbles start to form, or the kernels start to move and spin, it's hot enough. Pour in the rest of the kernels, put the lid on top of the saucepan and wait.

3 Once the corn starts popping, use oven mitts or kitchen towels to hold onto the handle of your saucepan and, keeping the lid on, shake the pan to ensure the heat is popping the kernels evenly.

4 Once the popping stops, take the saucepan off the heat, lift the lid and pour the chocolate over the top. Sprinkle with salt to taste, pop the lid back on and shake so that the chocolate spreads all around. (Alternatively, you can pour the popcorn into a bowl, then drizzle the chocolate on top.

Matilda mud cake

Serves 16

Chocolate cake is pretty much irresistible. And this one is as nutritious as it is delicious. Our recipe is inspired by one of our favourite childhood movies, *Matilda*. We love the movie because it's magical and a little rebellious at the same time, just like this cake. This is amazingly rich, but is completely refined sugar free. It's our go-to for all kinds of special occasions, so it's boyfriend and family approved too! Make this your own by topping it with any fruit you like. And make it gluten-free by replacing the spelt flour with a gluten-free flour.

CAKE

⅓ cup (75 g) coconut oil

½ cup (150 g) rice malt syrup

½ cup (60 g) wholemeal spelt flour

1½ cups (150 g) almond meal

½ cup (55 g) raw cacao powder

⅛ tsp salt

1 tsp baking powder

½ cup (125 ml) almond milk

3 large eggs, whisked

1 tsp vanilla extract

ICING

½ cup (110 g) coconut oil

¼ cup (30 g) raw cacao powder

⅓ cup (60 g) pitted and roughly chopped medjool dates

1. Preheat the oven to 180°C (350°F) and line a 23 cm (9 inch) cake tin with baking paper.

2. In a small saucepan over medium heat, melt the coconut oil and rice malt syrup.

3. In a large bowl, mix together the flour, almond meal, cacao powder and salt.

4. Stir the mixture from the saucepan through the dry mixture. Add the almond milk, eggs and vanilla extract and mix until combined.

5. Pour into the tin and bake for 20-25 minutes or until cooked through. Allow the cake to cool before icing.

6. In a blender or food processor, pulse the icing ingredients with ¼ cup (60 ml) hot water until smooth. Pour over the cake.

7. Store in an airtight container for 3-4 days.

Radical rocky road
Serves 16

Not only does this recipe look dreamy, but it tastes almost too good to be true. It's one of our absolute favourites, but it's also one of the easiest and quickest recipes to make – there isn't much washing up and there's no baking time. You just need 2 hours for it to set, so you could literally make it before dinner and it will be ready for you afterwards! If you to speed things up even more, pour it into a larger dish to increase the surface area and make the Rocky Road thinner. Feel free to change the ingredients to your favourite nut or dried fruit. Warning: this is super-addictive.

½ cup (110 g) coconut oil

3 Tbsp almond butter

¼ cup (75 g) rice malt syrup

½ cup (55 g) raw cacao powder

1 tsp maca powder (optional)

1 tsp vanilla extract

1 tsp bee pollen (optional)

1 cup (155 g) almonds, roughly chopped (or hazelnuts also work well)

½ cup (15 g) puffed rice (or puffed spelt or puffed millet)

½ cup (60 g) goji berries

½ cup (30 g) coconut flakes

¼ cup (60 g) cacao nibs

1 Line a large baking tray with baking paper, letting it hang over the sides for easy removal.

2 In a small saucepan over low heat, melt the coconut oil (if solid). Add the almond butter, syrup, cacao powder, maca, vanilla and pollen, stirring well until it is combined. Remove from the heat.

3 Mix together the almonds, puffed rice, goji berries, coconut flakes and cacao nibs in a bowl.

4 Add the liquid ingredients to the bowl, stir well then spread the mixture over the prepared tray. Set in the freezer for 2 hours.

5 Store in an airtight container in the freezer for up to 3 weeks.

note: We love bee pollen; it is full of vitamins and minerals and adds a special spark to the rocky road

Coconut and berry cookies

Makes 12

There is something delicious about the combination of coconut and raspberry – and even more delicious when it's in cookie form! These are the perfect healthy addition to afternoon tea or for after dinner. They're decadent and remind us of the rich raspberry and coconut cake we had as a treat as kids, but in a healthier, crunchier version with no added refined sugar.

1 cup (100 g) almond meal

½ cup (75 g) gluten-free flour

½ cup (35 g) shredded coconut

1 tsp baking powder

1 tsp vanilla extract

3 Tbsp rice malt syrup

¼ cup (55 g) coconut oil

2 Tbsp almond butter

2 Tbsp Greek yoghurt

½ cup (60 g) raspberries

1 Preheat the oven to 180°C (350°F). Line a baking tray with baking paper.

2 Mix together the almond meal, gluten-free flour, shredded coconut and baking powder.

3 Add the vanilla extract, rice malt syrup, coconut oil, almond butter and Greek yoghurt and mix well.

4 Gently fold the raspberries through the mixture.

5 Spoon 1 tablespoon dough at a time onto the baking tray and flatten into rounds. Bake in the oven for 12-14 minutes, or until browned.

6 Leave to cool for 15-20 minutes before serving.

Brilliant zucchini brownies

Makes 12

Yep, that says 'ZUCCHINI'! But never fear, you will barely be able to tell it's in there. Zucchinis are awesome to use in baking because they're subtle in flavour, have great nutritional value and give these healthy brownies a beautiful moist texture. These are just like traditional brownies, only healthy. And who doesn't love brownies? These are one of our family favourites.

1 zucchini (courgette)

2 eggs, lightly beaten

1 tsp vanilla extract

⅓ cup (100 g) rice malt syrup

¼ cup (55 g) coconut oil

1 tsp baking powder

½ cup (55 g) cacao powder

Pinch of sea salt

1 cup (100 g) almond meal

2 Tbsp nut butter

1   Preheat the oven to 180°C (350°F) and line a small square baking tray with baking paper.

2   Grate the zucchini and leave to strain in a colander. Squeeze out the moisture with your hands, then pat dry with paper towel.

3   Mix together the zucchini, eggs, vanilla extract, rice malt syrup and coconut oil in a bowl.

4   Add the baking powder, cacao powder, sea salt, almond meal and nut butter and mix until combined.

5   Pour into the baking tray and bake for 15–18 minutes until golden brown and cooked through (a knife should come out clean). Cut into 12 pieces and serve.

Cleaner ice cream

Serves 2

Healthy ice cream is extremely easy
and seriously delicious. If you keep
some frozen fruit in the freezer you
can make this any time you get a
craving. This one is a staple dessert
in our households.

1 cup (315 g) chopped mango,
  frozen (around 1 large mango)

1 banana, chopped and frozen

2 heaped Tbsp natural Greek
  yoghurt

A dash of almond milk

1 Add all the ingredients to a food
   processor and blend until smooth.

2 Serve immediately, or transfer to
   an airtight container and store in
   the freezer.

Creamy choc mousse

Serves 2

We can't help loving chocolate. This mousse will satisfy your tastebuds, but because of the healthy fats from the avocado and coconut milk, it's great for your belly and your body.

1 avocado
½ cup (55 g) cacao powder
¼ cup (60 ml) maple syrup
½ tsp vanilla extract
½ cup (125 ml) coconut milk
3 medjool dates, pitted
Raspberries, to serve

1 Combine all the ingredients in a food processor or blender. Add sea salt to taste and ½ cup (125 ml) water. Blend until smooth.

2 Transfer to a bowl and refrigerate for 1-2 hours to set.

3 Serve with raspberries or store in the fridge in a sealed container for up to 3 days.

Bugs Bunny muffins

Makes 12

It's a healthy twist on classic
carrot cake! If you're not into
fruit, but still want to enjoy a
healthy, slightly sweet muffin,
these *widdle wabbits* are for you.

2 eggs, lightly beaten
2 cups (310 g) grated carrot
½ cup (125 ml) almond milk
½ cup (130 g) Greek yoghurt
1 tsp vanilla extract
⅓ cup (115 g) rice malt syrup
1 cup (100 g) almond meal
1 cup (150 g) gluten-free flour
1 tsp baking powder
1 tsp cinnamon

1 Preheat the oven to 180°C (350°F)
   and line a medium muffin tray with
   12 patty pans or baking paper.

2 Mix together the eggs, carrot,
   almond milk, Greek yoghurt,
   vanilla and rice malt syrup.

3 Add the almond meal, flour, baking
   powder and cinnamon and mix until
   combined.

4 Spoon into the patty pans and bake
   for 20-24 minutes or until golden
   brown and cooked through.

5 Cool for at least 10 minutes
   before serving. Keep in an
   airtight container for 3 days.

Trixy bikkies

Makes 15

Seriously, what a perfect combination of chocolate, caramel and crunchy biscuit! This is a tribute to one of our absolute fave choccie bars when we were growing up — we just had to create a healthier, refined sugar-free version to make at home. We love whipping these up on special occasions to enjoy with friends and family. They're always a hit.

CARAMEL LAYER

1 cup (160 g) medjool dates, pitted and soaked in warm water

1 Tbsp tahini

BISCUIT LAYER

½ cup (50 g) almond meal

½ cup (75 g) gluten-free flour

¼ cup (55 g) coconut oil

1 tsp vanilla extract

1 Tbsp rice malt syrup

CHOCOLATE LAYER

½ cup (110 g) coconut oil

1 tsp vanilla extract

3 Tbsp almond butter

¼ cup (90 g) rice malt syrup

½ cup (55 g) raw cacao powder

1 Preheat the oven to 180°C (350°F) and line a medium-sized square baking tray with baking paper.

2 To make the caramel layer, mix the dates and tahini in a blender or food processor, with ½ cup (125 mL) water and sea salt to taste. Transfer the mixture to an airtight container and freeze for at least 40 minutes.

3 To make the biscuit layer, mix together all the ingredients to form a doughy mixture. Roll out the dough into a square about 3 mm thick and line the baking tray. Bake for 7–10 minutes or until golden brown. Remove from the oven and cool in the tin.

4 To make the chocolate layer, melt the coconut oil (if solid) and blend in a food processor or blender with the remaining ingredients until smooth.

5 Once the biscuit and caramel have both cooled, pour the caramel on top of the biscuit layer in the tray, then pour the chocolate layer on top. Freeze for at least 3–4 hours (or ideally overnight) before slicing into small snack-sized pieces.

6 Store in an airtight container in the freezer for up to 2 weeks.

Index

Published in 2018 by Murdoch Books,
an imprint of Allen & Unwin
Reprinted 2018, 2019(twice)

Murdoch Books Australia
83 Alexander Street,
Crows Nest NSW 2065
Phone: +61 (0)2 8425 0100
murdochbooks.com.au
info@murdochbooks.com.au

Murdoch Books UK
Ormond House, 26-27 Boswell Street,
London, WC1N 3JZ
Phone: +44 (0) 20 8785 5995
murdochbooks.co.uk
info@murdochbooks.co.uk

For Corporate Orders & Custom
Publishing contact our
business development team at
salesenquiries@murdochbooks.com.au

Publisher: Jane Morrow
Editorial Manager: Jane Price
Design Manager: Madeleine Kane
Editor: Kalya Ryan
Designer: Aileen Lord
Cover design: Estee Sarsfield
Photography: Ren Pidgeon, cover,
pages 1-141 and page 162 top;
Cath Muscat, pages 142-221 and page 30
Styling: Vanessa Austin
Food for photography: Ross Dobson
Production Director: Lou Playfair

ISBN 978 1 76052 385 5 Australia
ISBN 978 1 76063 463 6 UK

A cataloguing-in-publication entry
is available from the catalogue of
the National Library of Australia at
nla.gov.au
A catalogue record for this book is
available from the British Library

Colour reproduction by Splitting Image
Colour Studio, Clayton, Victoria
Printed by 1010 Printing Co Ltd, China

MEASURES GUIDE: We have used
Australian 20 ml (4 teaspoon)
tablespoon measures. If you are using
a smaller European 15 ml (3 teaspoon)
tablespoon, add an extra teaspoon of
the ingredient for each tablespoon.